Prophets III

HOSEA, JOEL, AMOS, OBADIAH, JONAH, MICAH, NAHUM, HABAKKUK, ZEPHANIAH, HAGGAI, ZECHARIAH, MALACHI

WILLIAM A. ANDERSON, DMIN, PHD

Liguori
LIGUORI, MISSOURI

Imprimi Potest:
Harry Grile, CSsR, Provincial
Denver Province, The Redemptorists

Printed with Ecclesiastical Permission and Approved for Private or Instructional Use

Nihil Obstat: Rev. Msgr. Kevin Michael Quirk, JCD, JV
          Censor Librorum

Imprimatur: + Michael J. Bransfield
          Bishop of Wheeling-Charleston [West Virginia]
          December 26, 2013

Published by Liguori Publications
Liguori, Missouri 63057

To order, visit Liguori.org or call 800-325-9521.

Library of Congress Cataloging-in-Publication Data

Anderson, William Angor, 1937-
  Prophets III : Hosea, Joel, Amos, Obadiah, Jonah, Micah, Nahum, Habakkuk, Zephaniah, Haggai, Zechariah, Malachi / William A. Anderson, DMin, PhD.—First Edition.
    pages cm
  ISBN 978-0-7648-2137-0
  1. Bible. Minor prophets—Textbooks. I. Title.
  BS1560.A77 2014
  224'.90071—dc23
                    2014006894
  p ISBN 978-0-7648-2137-0
  e ISBN 978-0-7648-6924-2

Liguori Publications, a nonprofit corporation, is an apostolate of The Redemptorists. To learn more about The Redemptorists, visit Redemptorists.com.

Printed in the United States of America
18 17 16 15 14 / 5 4 3 2 1
First Edition

Contents

NOTE: The length of each Bible section varies. Group leaders should com-bine sections as needed to fit the number of sessions in their program.

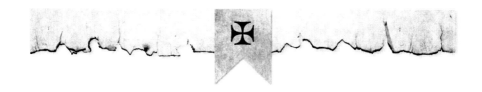

Dedication

THIS SERIES is lovingly dedicated to the memory of my parents, Angor and Kathleen Anderson, in gratitude for all they shared with all who knew them, especially my siblings and me.

Acknowledgments

BIBLE STUDIES and reflections depend on the help of others who read the manuscript and make suggestions. I am especially indebted to Sister Anne Francis Bartus, CSJ, DMin, whose vast experience and knowledge were very helpful in bringing this series to its final form.

Introduction to
Liguori Catholic Bible Study

READING THE BIBLE can be daunting. It's a complex book, and many a person of goodwill has tried to read the Bible and ended up putting it down in utter confusion. It helps to have a companion, and *Liguori Catholic Bible Study* is a solid one. Over the course of this series, you'll learn about biblical messages, themes, personalities, and events and understand how the books of the Bible rose out of the need to address new situations.

Across the centuries, people of faith have asked, "Where is God in this moment?" Millions of Catholics look to the Bible for encouragement in their journey of faith. Wisdom teaches us not to undertake Bible study alone, disconnected from the Church that was given Scripture to share and treasure. When used as a source of prayer and thoughtful reflection, the Bible comes alive.

Your choice of a Bible-study program should be dictated by what you want to get out of it. One goal of *Liguori Catholic Bible Study* is to give readers greater familiarity with the Bible's structure, themes, personalities, and message. But that's not enough. This program will also teach you to use Scripture in your prayer. God's message is as compelling and urgent today as ever, but we get only part of the message when it's memorized and stuck in our head. It's meant for the entire person—physical, emotional, and spiritual.

We're baptized into life with Christ, and we're called to live more fully with Christ today as we practice the values of justice, peace, forgiveness, and community. God's new covenant was written on the hearts of the people of Israel; we, their spiritual descendants, are loved that intimately by God today. *Liguori Catholic Bible Study* will draw you closer to God, in whose image and likeness we are fashioned.

Group and Individual Study

The *Liguori Catholic Bible Study* series is intended for group and individual study and prayer. This series gives you the tools to start a study group. Gathering two or three people in a home or announcing the meeting of a Bible-study group in a parish or community can bring surprising results. Each lesson in this series contains a section to help groups study, reflect, pray, and share biblical reflections. Each lesson but the first also has a second section for individual study.

Many people who want to learn more about the Bible don't know where to begin. This series gives them a place to start and helps them continue until they're familiar with all the books of the Bible.

Bible study can be a lifelong project, always enriching those who wish to be faithful to God's Word. When people complete a study of the whole Bible, they can begin again, making new discoveries with each new adventure into the Word of God.

Lectio Divina
(Sacred Reading)

BIBLE STUDY isn't just a matter of gaining intellectual knowledge of the Bible; it's also about gaining a greater understanding of God's love and concern for creation. The purpose of reading and knowing the Bible is to enrich our relationship with God. God loves us and gave us the Bible to illustrate that love. In his April 12, 2013, address before the Pontifical Biblical Commission, Pope Francis stressed that "the Church's life and mission are founded on the Word of God which is the soul of theology and at the same time inspires the whole of Christian life."

The Meaning of *Lectio Divina*

Lectio divina is a Latin expression that means "divine or sacred reading." The process for *lectio divina* consists of Scripture readings, reflection, and prayer. Many clergy, religious, and laity use *lectio divina* in their daily spiritual reading to develop a closer and more loving relationship with God. Learning about Scripture has as its purpose the living of its message, which demands a period of reflection on Scripture passages.

Prayer and *Lectio Divina*

Prayer is a necessary element for the practice of *lectio divina*. The entire process of reading and reflecting is a prayer. It's not merely an intellectual pursuit; it's also a spiritual one. Page 15 includes an opening prayer for gathering one's thoughts before moving on to the passages in each section. This prayer may be used privately or in a group. For those who use the book for daily spiritual reading, the prayer for each section may be repeated each day. Some may wish to keep a journal of each day's meditation.

Pondering the Word of God

Lectio divina is the ancient Christian spiritual practice of reading the holy Scriptures with intentionality and devotion. This practice helps Christians center themselves and descend to the level of the heart to enter an inner quiet space, finding God.

This sacred reading is distinct from reading for knowledge or information, and it's more than the pious practice of spiritual reading. It is the practice of opening ourselves to the action and inspiration of the Holy Spirit. As we intentionally focus on and become present to the inner meaning of the Scripture passage, the Holy Spirit enlightens our minds and hearts. We come to the text willing to be influenced by a deeper meaning that lies within the words and thoughts we ponder.

In this space, we open ourselves to be challenged and changed by the inner meaning we experience. We approach the text in a spirit of faith and obedience as a disciple ready to be taught by the Holy Spirit. As we savor the sacred text, we let go of our usual control of how we expect God to act in our lives and surrender our heart and conscience to the flow of the divine (*divina*) through the reading (*lectio*).

The fundamental principle of *lectio divina* leads us to understand the profound mystery of the Incarnation, "The Word became flesh," not only in history but also within us.

Praying *Lectio* Today

Before you begin, relax your body and maintain a posture of prayer (back straight, eyes shut, feet flat on the floor). Then practice these four simple actions:

1. Read a passage from Scripture or the daily Mass readings. This is known as *lectio*. (If the Word of God is read aloud, the hearers listen attentively.)

2. Pray the selected passage with attention as you listen for a specific meaning that comes to mind. Once again, the reading is listened to or silently read and reflected or meditated on. This is known as *meditatio*.

3. The exercise becomes active. Pick a word, sentence, or idea that surfaces from your consideration of the chosen text. Does the reading remind you of a person, place, or experience? If so, pray about it. Compose your thoughts and reflection into a simple word or phrase. This prayer-thought will help you remove distractions during the *lectio*. This exercise is called *oratio*.

4. In silence, with your eyes closed, quiet yourself and become conscious of your breathing. Let your thoughts, feelings, and concerns fade as you consider the selected passage in the previous step (*oratio*). If you're distracted, use your prayer word to help you return to silence. This is *contemplatio*.

This exercise can take as long as you want, but in the context of this Bible study, 10 to 20 minutes should be sufficient.

Many teachers of prayer call contemplation the prayer of resting in God, a prelude to losing oneself in the presence of God. Scripture is transformed in our hearing as we pray and allow our hearts to unite intimately with the Lord. The Word truly takes on flesh, and this time it is manifested in our flesh.

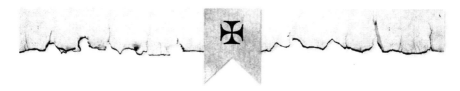

How to Use This
Bible-Study Companion

THE BIBLE, along with the commentaries and reflections found in this study, will help participants become familiar with the Scripture texts and lead them to reflect more deeply on the texts' messages. At the end of this study, participants will have a firm grasp of the books of the minor prophets, becoming therefore more aware of the spiritual nourishment these books offer. This study is not only an intellectual adventure, it's also a spiritual one. The reflections lead participants into their own journey with the Scripture readings.

Context

When the authors wrote and edited the books of the minor prophets, they were living at a time when other nations were invading and ravaging the land of the Israelites. To help readers learn about each passage in relation to those around it, each lesson begins with an overview that puts the Scripture passages into context.

Part 1: Group Study

To give participants a comprehensive study of the minor prophets, the book is divided into seven lessons. Lesson 1 is group study only; Lessons 2 through 7 are divided into Part 1, group study, and Part 2, individual study. For example, Lesson 2 covers the Book of Hosea 4 through 14. The study group reads and discusses only chapters 4 through 5:14 (Part 1). Participants privately read and reflect on chapters 5:15 through 14 (Part 2).

Group study may or may not include *lectio divina*. With *lectio divina*, the group meets for ninety minutes using the first format on page 13. Without *lectio divina*, the group meets for one hour using the format at the bottom of page 13, and participants are urged to privately read the *lectio divina* section at the end of Part 1. It contains additional reflections on the Scripture passages studied during the group session that will take participants even further into the passages.

Part 2: Individual Study

The passages not covered in Part 1 are divided into shorter components, one to be studied each day. Participants who don't belong to a study group can use the lessons for private sacred reading. They may choose to reflect on one Scripture passage per day, making it possible for a clearer understanding of the Scripture passages used in their *lectio divina* (sacred reading).

A PROCESS FOR SACRED READING

Liguori Publications has designed this study to be user-friendly and manageable. However, group dynamics and leaders vary. We're not trying to keep the Holy Spirit from working in your midst, thus we suggest you decide beforehand which format works best for your group. If you have limited time, you could study the Bible as a group and save prayer and reflection for personal time.

However, if your group wishes to digest and feast on sacred Scripture through both prayer and study, we recommend you spend closer to ninety minutes each week by gathering to study and pray with Scripture. *Lectio divina* (see page 8) is an ancient contemplative prayer form that moves readers from the head to the heart in meeting the Lord. We strongly suggest using this prayer form whether in individual or group study.

GROUP-STUDY FORMATS

1. Bible Study With *Lectio Divina*

About ninety minutes of group study

- ✠ Gathering and opening prayer (3–5 minutes)
- ✠ Read each Scripture passage aloud (5 minutes)
- ✠ Silently review the commentary and prepare to discuss it with the group (3–5 minutes)
- ✠ Discuss the Scripture passage along with the commentary and reflection (30 minutes)
- ✠ Read each Scripture passage aloud a second time, followed by quiet time for meditation and contemplation (5 minutes)
- ✠ Spend some time in prayer with the selected passage. Group participants will slowly read the Scripture passage a third time in silence, listening for the voice of God as they read (10–20 minutes)
- ✠ Shared reflection (10–15 minutes)
- ✠ Closing prayer (3–5 minutes)

To become acquainted with lectio divina, *see page 8.*

2. Bible Study

About one hour of group study

- ✠ Gathering and opening prayer (3–5 minutes)
- ✠ Read each Scripture passage aloud (5 minutes)
- ✠ Silently review the commentary and prepare to discuss it with the group (3–5 minutes)
- ✠ Discuss the Scripture passage along with the commentary and reflections (40 minutes)
- ✠ Closing prayer (3–5 minutes)

Notes to the Leader

✠ Bring a copy of the *New American Bible,* revised edition.

✠ Plan which sections will be covered each week of your Bible study.

✠ Read the material in advance of each session.

✠ Establish written ground rules. (Example: We won't keep you longer than ninety minutes; don't dominate the sharing by arguing or debating.)

✠ Meet in an appropriate and welcoming gathering space (church building, meeting room, house).

✠ Provide name tags and perhaps use a brief icebreaker for the first meeting; ask participants to introduce themselves.

✠ Mark the Scripture passage(s) that will be read during the session.

✠ Decide how you would like the Scripture to be read aloud (whether by one or multiple readers).

✠ Use a clock or watch.

✠ Provide extra Bibles (or copies of the Scripture passages) for participants who don't bring their Bible.

✠ Ask participants to read "Introduction: Prophets III" (page 16) before the first session.

✠ Tell participants which passages to study and urge them to read the passages and commentaries before the meeting.

✠ If you opt to use the *lectio divina* format, familiarize yourself with this prayer form ahead of time.

Notes to the Participants

✠ Bring a copy of the *New American Bible,* revised edition.

✠ Read "Introduction: Prophets III" (page 16) before the first session.

✠ Read the Scripture passages and commentaries before each session.

✠ Be prepared to share and listen respectfully. (This is not a time to debate beliefs or argue.)

Opening Prayer

Leader: O God, come to my assistance.

Response: O Lord, make haste to help me.

Leader: Glory be to the Father, and to the Son, and to the Holy Spirit...

Response: ...as it was in the beginning, is now, and ever shall be, world without end. Amen.

Leader: Christ is the vine and we are the branches. As branches linked to Jesus, the vine, we are called to recognize that the Scriptures are always being fulfilled in our lives. It is the living Word of God living on in us. Come, Holy Spirit, fill the hearts of your faithful and kindle in us the fire of your divine wisdom, knowledge, and love.

Response: Open our minds and hearts as we study your great love for us as shown in the Bible.

Reader: (Open your Bible to the assigned Scripture(s) and read in a paced, deliberate manner. Pause for one minute, listening for a word, phrase, or image that you may use in your *lectio divina* practice.)

Closing Prayer

Leader: Let us pray as Jesus taught us.

Response: Our Father...

Leader: Lord, inspire us with your Spirit as we study your Word in the Bible. Be with us this day and every day as we strive to know you and serve you and to love as you love. We believe that through your goodness and love, the Spirit of the Lord is truly upon us. Allow the words of the Bible, your Word, to capture us and inspire us to live as you live and to love as you love.

Response: Amen.

Leader: May the divine assistance remain with us always.

Response: In the name of the Father, and of the Son, and of the Holy Spirit. Amen.

Prophets III

HOSEA, JOEL, AMOS, OBADIAH, JONAH, MICAH,

NAHUM, HABAKKUK, ZEPHANIAH,

HAGGAI, ZECHARIAH, MALACHI

Read this overview before the first session.

The Word of the Lord came to the Israelites through the prophets. Because the prophets had to warn the people about the destruction they would soon endure, the prophets were often disliked and threatened. Totally dedicated to the Lord and the covenant, the true prophets courageously conveyed the Word of the Lord to the people despite rejection, persecution, and possible death.

Major and Minor Prophets

Among the prophetic books, there are four major and twelve minor prophetical writings. The terms major and minor refer to the length of the writings. The major prophets include the books of Isaiah, Jeremiah, Ezekiel, and Daniel. The minor prophets include the writings of Hosea, Joel, Amos, Obadiah, Jonah, Micah, Nahum, Habakkuk, Zephaniah, Haggai, Zechariah, and Malachi.

This volume of the *Liguori Catholic Bible Study* series will examine the writings of the twelve minor prophets.

Historical Perspective

The Syro-Ephraimite War: In 735–734 BC, Syria and Ephraim feared the impending invasion of the powerful Assyrian army and joined together to fight the Assyrians. When speaking about the northern kingdom of Israel, the prophets often used the name Ephraim, the largest city in the northern kingdom, to represent Israel. Syria was also known as Aram. Leaders of the Syrian-Israel alliance asked King Ahaz of Judah to engage his forces to help the alliance fend off the Assyrians, but Ahaz refused.

The kings of Syria and Israel, unhappy with King Ahaz's refusal, fought against Judah with the hope of removing the king and placing a king more favorable to their cause on the throne. At the beginning of the invasion, Judah lost many warriors and called on the Assyrians for help. With the help of the Assyrians, Judah was able to successfully defend itself against the Syro-Ephraimite force. But the alliance with Assyria left Judah as a vassal of Assyria, compelling Judah to pay an excessive tribute to the Assyrians.

Assyrian Domination: In 721 BC, the Assyrian army conquered and destroyed the northern kingdom of Israel, forcing many of its inhabitants to flee to the southern kingdom of Judah. Most of those who did not escape from Israel were sent into exile in other lands conquered by the Assyrians, where they intermarried with the natives of the area. Exiles from other countries were brought to the northern kingdom and forced to intermarry with the Israelites who remained in the north.

Babylonian Domination: The Babylonians (Chaldeans) became a dominant power during the seventh and sixth centuries before Christ. The Assyrian Empire was no longer a feared powerful empire, and the Babylonians had become a constant threat and thorn in the side of the cities of Judah. The powerful Babylonians forced Judah into paying an excessive tribute after invading the area. In an attempt to break away from the control of the Babylonians, the king of Judah incited a rebellion against the Babylonians, leading the Babylonian nation to invade and devastate the land in 587 BC. The destruction of Jerusalem, its Temple, and the cities of Judah was a horrible and frightening experience for the people of Judah who survived. The Babylonians led many people of Jerusalem and the cities of Judah into exile in Babylon. Others managed to flee to neighboring countries where they were often not welcomed.

In 538 BC, Cyrus the Great of Persia defeated the Babylonians, and the exiled people of Judah were allowed to return to their homeland from all the countries in which they lived. Many returned, while many others remained in the country they had known since birth. During the period after their return from exile, the people of Judah rebuilt the Jerusalem Temple, their most sacred place of worship.

The Book of Hosea (I)

HOSEA 1–3

I will betroth you to me forever: I will betroth you to me with justice, and with judgment, with loyalty and with compassion; I will betroth you to me with fidelity, and you shall know the LORD (2:21–22).

Opening Prayer (SEE PAGE 15)

Context

Hosea 1—3 During the last years of the reign of King Jeroboam II (783–743 BC), Hosea began his ministry in the northern kingdom. At the time, Israel was enjoying a period of economic prosperity and political power, while Assyria was becoming a powerful nation, attempting to expand its kingdom by conquering other nations, among them the northern kingdom of Israel. After the reign of Jeroboam II ended in 743 BC, Israel experienced a period of instability and decay during which time several of the kings succeeding Jeroboam were assassinated. Although the prophet foresaw the threat of an Assyrian invasion at the end of his life, he apparently died before it actually took place around 722 to 721 BC.

The Lord instructs Hosea to marry a prostitute and have children with her. The prostitute and the children represent Israel. The children receive names symbolizing their rejection by the Lord, but in the end the Lord will relent and proclaim them again to be God's people. Although Gomer (Israel) prostituted herself by worshiping false gods, the Lord will lure her back.

PART 1: GROUP STUDY (HOSEA 1—3)

Read aloud Hosea 1—3:5.

1 Marriage to Gomer

Although Hosea preached in the northern kingdom of Israel, his speeches were brought to the southern kingdom of Judah, most likely after the Assyrian invasion, where a later editor wrote down Hosea's speeches and inserted some passages of his own into the text. In the opening lines naming the kings who reigned while Hosea was prophesying, the list of the kings begins with the kings of Judah, not the kings of Israel in the north. The choice of naming Judean kings over the kings of Israel is a further indication an author from the southern kingdom penned the speeches of Hosea. At the end of the list, the editor does add the name of King Jeroboam II of Israel.

The author begins his message with the usual introduction to prophetic speech: "The word of the LORD that came to Hosea" (1:1). The father of Hosea is named as Beeri. When naming an important person in Israel, the father's name is usually given, but it is often difficult to clearly know the identity of the father.

The Lord directs Hosea to take a prostitute as his wife. The text also indicates Hosea is to take the children of the prostitute, which is a reference to the children Hosea will beget with his wife. The image of a prostitute is a symbolic image representing the nation of Israel, which has prostituted itself by worshiping false gods. The children of the prostitute refer to the people of Israel who worship false gods.

Hosea marries a prostitute named Gomer, who gives birth to her firstborn, a son. Identifying Gomer as a prostitute indicates she rejected the Lord for the worship of a false god. The Lord instructs Hosea to name the child "Jezreel," meaning "God sows," a reference to the afflictions the

Lord casts on the people of Israel. In 842 BC, King Jehu became king of Israel after killing King Joram of Israel at a place named "Jezreel" (see 2 Kings 9—10). In the Book of Hosea, the Lord foretells a punishment for the house of Jehu and the destruction of the northern kingdom of Israel in the valley of Jezreel. The Lord's words concerning the fall of the house of Jehu were fulfilled after Zechariah, the son of Jeroboam II, was killed (see 2 Kings 15:8–13).

Gomer then bears a daughter and the Lord instructs Hosea to name the child "Not-Pitied," a sign the Lord will no longer pity the house of Israel and will spurn her. An editor in Judah will later add that the Lord will feel pity for the house of Judah and will save Judah, not, however, in combat. The Lord does not need human weapons to defeat an enemy, as shown earlier in 2 Kings, when an angel of the Lord strikes dead 185,000 Assyrian warriors (see 2 Kings 19:35).

Gomer conceives a third child, a son whom the Lord directs Hosea to name, "Not-My-People," a sign the Lord had abandoned the people. In 1:9, the Lord states, "I am not 'I am' for you," which is in contrast to the words the Lord spoke to Moses when the Lord stated, "I will take you as my own people, and I will be your God; and you will know that I, the LORD, am your God" (Exodus 6:7).

2 Israel as the Lord's Spouse

The tone in this chapter changes from rejection to the promise of a future reception back into the Lord's good graces. The Lord repeats the promise made to Abraham, saying the members of the house of the Israelites will not be able to be counted and will be as numerous as "the sands of the seashore" (Genesis 22:17). The names given to the children of Gomer now refer to all of Israel.

The Lord then changes the names given to the children in the first chapter, changing the name of the offspring of Gomer from "Not-My-People" to "Children of the Living God." The people of Judah and Israel will unite and appoint a single leader for themselves, an apparent addition by an editor in Judah who was aware of the eventual unity of the people of the northern and southern kingdoms under a new leader. Just as Jezreel was a place of treachery in the past, it now becomes a place providing a day of unity for the nation. The offspring once named "Not-My-People" are now named "My People," and those named "Not-Pitied" are now named "Pitied."

The Lord continues to use the image of a marriage, declaring the mother of the children (Israel) is not the Lord's spouse but a prostitute who must remove all prostitution from herself. In worshiping false gods, she has divorced herself from the Lord. The Lord will strip the mother naked, a reference to the Lord's rejection of Israel, allowing the nation to return to the period when she was in the wilderness, a thirsty nation in an arid land. The Lord will allow her to die of thirst.

The Lord shall have no pity on Israel's children, who are the offspring of prostitution. She acted shamefully, going after lovers who provided bread and water, wool and flax, oil and drink. The text refers to the Israelite nation forgetting the support of the Lord and turning to others gods of Baal. The Lord surrounds her (Israel) with briars, builds a wall against her, and abandons her. Her lovers, because they do not exist, can provide nothing for her, and she will long to return to her first husband, where she had a better life. In many passages found in prophetic writings, the lovers can refer to foreign nations supporting the Israelites or the worship of false gods.

The nation forgot the Lord provided her with grain, wine, oil, and the silver and gold they used for the ornamentation of the false god, the Baal idol. The Lord will take back the grain and wine, a reference to a drought and, lacking wool and flax, they will have no means of providing clothing for themselves. The nation will stand in shame, in full view of her lovers, with no one powerful enough to free her from the wrath of the Lord, meaning the weakened state of Israel will leave the inhabitants vulnerable to invading armies.

Since the land became a waste and the agricultural gifts like grain, wine, and oil cease, Israel's seasonal feasts will end. The decaying vines and the fig trees will be devoured by wild animals. The Lord will punish the people of Israel who dressed elegantly to offer incense to Baal while forgetting the Lord of Israel.

The Lord, however, will relent, luring Israel to return to true worship.

Leading her into the wilderness, the Lord will speak convincing words to her and return her vineyards to her, bringing her to the valley of Achor, which was ordinarily used to designate a valley of doom but used here to express the idea of a valley of hope. On the day she responds in the same manner as she did when she came from the land of Egypt, she will call the Lord "my husband" and never again refer to the Lord as "my baal." In this case, "baal" does not refer to a false god, but it means lord and master, often used by women when speaking of their husbands. It was never used in reference to the Lord God due to its use in referring to the fertility gods.

The Lord will make a covenant with all of creation, destroying all weapons of war and enabling the nation of the Israelites to reside in safety. She will be betrothed to the Lord forever, with justice, judgment, loyalty, compassion, and fidelity. Then they shall know the Lord. In using the word "know," the author claims the intimacy of this relationship will be like one between a husband and wife.

The earth shall be in perfect harmony, as it was at the time of creation, with each part serving the other. The Lord will have pity on the child once named "Not-Pitied," and the Lord will change the name "Not-My-People" to "You are my people," and the child will say, "My God."

3 Hosea and His Wife Are Reunited

In chapter three, Hosea begins to speak in the first person. The depiction of his relationship with the prostitute continues to point to the Lord's relationship with Israel. The Lord instructs Hosea to go and love the woman who commits adultery. He is to love her in the same way the Lord loves the Israelites who turned to other gods and love raisin cakes. The raisin cakes were offered in worship to the fertility goddess, Asherah. Since Hosea divorced the prostitute (Israel), he must now reacquire her with a marriage offering of fifteen pieces of silver, along with a homer and a lethech of barley. A homer of barley was a mule load amounting to about ten bushels, and a lethech of barley was a half-homer.

Hosea instructs his wife to wait for many days, as he too will wait for many days. He urges her not to prostitute herself or allow herself to belong to any other man. The waiting refers to the time in exile when the people are without a king and without an opportunity for Temple worship. After this period of waiting, the Israelites will seek the Lord, their God, and a successor to the line of David as their king. In the last days, when their exile ends, they will return in awe to the Lord and the Lord's bounty.

Review Questions

1. What is the meaning of the symbolism in the story of Hosea's marriage to Gomer?
2. Why does the Lord have a change of mind concerning the Lord's pity for the Israelites?
3. Who are the lovers the Lord warns against?
4. What is the meaning of the passage when the Lord tells the people they must wait for the Lord for many days?

Closing Prayer (SEE PAGE 15)

Pray the closing prayer now or after *lectio divina*.

Lectio Divina (SEE PAGE 8)

Relax your body and maintain a posture of prayer (back straight, eyes shut, feet flat on the floor). This exercise can take as long as you want, but in the context of this Bible study, 10 to 20 minutes should be sufficient.

The meditations that follow are provided only to help group participants use this prayer form, but note that *lectio* is intended to bring one to a place of prayerful contemplation where the Word of God speaks to the hearer from his or her heart. (See page 8 for further instruction.)

Marriage to Gomer (1)

God warned the Israelites, who were represented by Gomer and her children, that the Lord would have no pity on them. Despite these dire words, many of the Israelites had hope the Lord would forgive them if they repented. Christians learn Christ the Lord always forgives, no matter how bad the sin, as long as people repent of their sinfulness. The Lord never reaches the point where forgiveness will not be given.

✠ *What can I learn from this passage?*

Israel as the Lord's Spouse (2)

A woman, who ran away from home at the age of seventeen, traveled to New York with the expectation life would be wonderful there. Unable to find a job, she eventually had to prostitute herself to raise money for food and shelter. By the time she was twenty-two, her life had become miserable.

One night, she stopped at a church building she often passed on her way "to work." She spoke to the pastor of the parish, who happened to be near the altar preparing for the next morning's liturgy, telling him her story. The pastor talked her into calling her family in Ohio. As a result of the call, her father came to New York, met with her, gave her a crushing and grateful hug and, in his joy, wept like a baby. Until that time, she had convinced herself the family had rejected her and no longer loved her. "On that day," she told some friends, "I experienced the power of love in my father's hug."

The Lord is like that father. No matter how much the Israelites sinned in worshiping other gods, the Lord's arms were always open to welcome them back with a loving embrace. The Lord does the same with us.

✠ *What can I learn from this passage?*

Hosea and His Wife Are Reunited (3)

Despite the sinfulness of the Israelites in worshiping false gods, the Lord foresees a day when they will return to the Lord, their God. History is filled with stories of saints who once were sinners. Saint Francis of Assisi lived a self-centered life until he decided to dedicate himself to the Lord. Saint Augustine lived a life centered on pleasure until his conversion and total dedication to the Lord. The Lord's prediction in Hosea, claiming the Israelites will turn back to the Lord, shows the world that great sinners can become great saints, like St. Augustine.

✠ *What can I learn from this passage?*

The Book of Hosea (II)

HOSEA 4–14

Who is wise enough to understand these things? Who is intelligent enough to know them? Straight are the paths of the LORD, the just walk in them, but sinners stumble in them (14:10).

Opening Prayer (SEE PAGE 15)

Context

Part 1: Hosea 4—5:14 The people of the northern kingdom of Israel break the commandments of the Lord, and the Lord punishes them with complete devastation. The people lack knowledge of God because the priests, who also lack this knowledge, did not fulfill their task and teach the people. Because the people turn to idol worship, the Lord punishes them.

Part 2: Hosea 5:15—14 The Lord desires loyalty from the Israelites, not sacrifice. When the Lord would have healed them and taken them back, they choose wickedness, making alliances with other nations and accepting the gods of other nations. They violate the covenant by worshiping idols made by human hands, thus prostituting themselves in the eyes of the Lord. The Lord will punish them for their sinfulness. Although the Lord cares for them like a loving parent, they become unfaithful and proud.

PART 1: GROUP STUDY (HOSEA 4—5:14)

Read aloud Hosea 4—5:14.

4 Guilt of the Nation

The author begins this passage by using the expression, "Hear the Word of the LORD," which indicates the Lord is about to proclaim oracles directed to Israel. The first oracle is against all the people of Israel, accusing them of lacking fidelity, loyalty, or knowledge of God, which resulted in their swearing, lying, murdering, stealing, and adultery. The people had to be aware of these sins, since they were obviously against the commandments God gave to Moses (see Exodus 20:1–17). As a result of the sinfulness of the people, the Lord will punish them by drying up the land and causing all those dwelling in the land to perish, including the beasts of the land, the birds of the sky, and the fish of the sea. The devastation shall envelop everything, on land, in the sky, and under the water.

The Lord's anger then turned against the priest and prophet of Israel whom the Lord accused of sinning day and night. Because of this sinfulness, the Lord will make an end to the priest's mother, which appears to be a reference to the end of the priestly line. Because both priest and prophet rejected knowledge of the Lord and damaged the life of the people by not instructing them about God, the Lord will reject the priest and prophet. The knowledge of God refers to knowledge of the law of God. Because the priest forgot the law of the Lord, the Lord will forget his children. Forgetting the law of the Lord means the priest knew the law, but chose to ignore it.

The more the priests multiplied, the more they sinned against the Lord. The Lord threatens to change their glory into shame. The meaning of the word "glory" in this passage is vague, referring either to the children or to the Lord whom they are rejecting.

The priests greedily "feed on the sin of [the Lord's] people" (4:8), literally eating the food offered as sacrifice and worshiping idols. The Lord will punish the priests, who are no better than the people. In their prostitution (their worship of false idols), the priests will eat without being satisfied and promote prostitution while receiving nothing in return. Because they abandoned the Lord in worshiping idols, they will find themselves unfulfilled. In their false worship, they drink wine, aged or newly pressed, leaving them without any understanding of the one true God, as though they were drunk. The passage warns the priests the more they worship false gods, the more their knowledge of the God of Israel will waste away.

The Lord accuses the priests of foolishly consulting an empty piece of wood or a wand used by sorcerers as a guide. In places of worship on mountaintops or in the shade of trees, they offer sacrifice. Their daughters prostitute themselves, and their daughters-in-law commit adultery, meaning all the people of Israel worship false gods. Using the image of daughters and daughters-in-law stresses the practice of the era of punishing women rather than men for sexual sins. Because the Israelites were not taught knowledge of God by the priests, the Lord will not hold the people responsible (daughters and daughters-in-law), but the Lord will punish the men (priests) who consort with Temple women. Consorting not only includes worship of a false god, but also sexual sharing as part of a fertility rite.

The Lord warns Israel not to think Judah is sharing in their prostitution, a sign the editor is writing from Judah. The Lord commands the people of Israel not to go to their shrines at Gilgal and Beth-aven, which were the shrines where the northern tribes worshiped the Lord and which have become places of idol worship.

The Lord tells the people of Israel they are not to use the expression, "As the Lord lives" (4:15), which was ordinarily used to support an oath. Since the people of Israel abandoned the Lord, they should not use this saying to support the truth of their oath. The Lord compares Israel to a stubborn cow that the Lord will not bring to pasture with lambs. Since the people show they love the shame of their prostitution more than honor, the Lord declares Ephraim is bound to idols. Ephraim, the largest tribe of the northern kingdom, is one of the names Hosea uses when referring to the kingdom of Israel. The Lord sadly declares the wind (spirit) and the altars of idolatry have captured the hearts of the people.

5:1–14 Upheaval in Israel

The Lord calls upon the leaders of Israel, the priests, the elders, and the king to listen to the Word of the Lord. They have the responsibility of exercising judgment on the people, not just juridical judgment, but the protection of the moral and religious life of the people. Instead of bringing right judgment, they have led the people into idolatry. The Lord names three places where the people of Israel practiced idolatry, namely Mizpah, Tabor, and Shittim. Because of their idol worship, the Lord will now punish all the people.

As a result of their prostitution, Ephraim and all of Israel are possessed with the spirit of idolatry. Since they no longer know the Lord, their deeds blind them from returning to the Lord. Their arrogance and sinfulness become a witness against them. The author writes that the Lord asserts Judah will fall with them. The people will bring their animals for sacrifice to the Lord, but they will discover the Lord has abandoned them. They have borne illegitimate children, who are born for idolatry. In other words, the practice of idolatry will pass on from parents to children. The feast of the new moon, which is ordinarily a time of celebration for the Israelites, will now be a time of ruin.

The Lord warns the people of the tribe of Benjamin to look behind them. The image of the people looking behind them appears to refer to a war between the northern and southern kingdoms known as the Syro-Ephraimite War (see "Introduction: Prophets III," page 16). The tribe of Benjamin ordinarily belonged to the kingdom of Judah, but it appears the northern tribe of Israel at some time annexed Benjamin into its kingdom. Benjamin, on the border between the northern and southern kingdoms, would be the first tribe attacked in a war between the two kingdoms. Toward the end of the Syro-Ephraimite War, Judah attacked the tribe of Benjamin, which belonged to the northern kingdom.

Since Assyria sought to conquer the northern kingdom of Israel, they willingly joined forces with Judah at the time of the Syro-Ephraimite War. After Judah protected itself against the forces of the north in the Syro-Ephraimite war, Assyria conquered and destroyed the northern kingdom in 721 BC. The Lord predicted Ephraim (Israel) would become a wasteland on the day the Lord punishes them.

Since Judah did not support Ephraim against the Assyrians, the Lord punished Judah because they became like those who move boundary lines. The boundaries of the tribes of the Israelites had become sacred to the Lord, and the Lord appears to blame Judah for not protecting the boundaries of Israel. In the Book of Deuteronomy, the Lord decreed those people cursed who moved a person's boundary markers (see Deuteronomy 27:17). Because Israel went after "filth" (false gods), the Lord also casts a severe judgment on them.

Before the Syro-Ephraimite war, Ephraim was a vassal of Assyria and was forced to pay tribute to Assyria. When Judah sought Assyria's help in fighting the Syro-Ephraimite war, Judah became a vassal of Assyria and had to pay tribute to Assyria. To the people of Israel and Judah, the Lord, like a lion tearing apart and carrying away its prey, was punishing both nations.

Review Questions

1. What are the sins of the people of the northern tribe of Israel?
2. How would you apply the idea "knowledge of God," as used in this text, to situations in the world today?
3. How have the priests sinned against the people?
4. Is the Lord fair by being more lenient in punishing the people (the daughters) than in punishing the priests (the men)?
5. Why did the Lord punish Ephraim and Judah?

Closing Prayer (SEE PAGE 15)

Pray the closing prayer now or after *lectio divina*.

Lectio Divina (SEE PAGE 8)

Relax your body and maintain a posture of prayer (back straight, eyes shut, feet flat on the floor). This exercise can take as long as you want, but in the context of this Bible study, 10 to 20 minutes should be sufficient.

The meditations that follow are provided only to help group participants use this prayer form, but note that *lectio* is intended to bring one to a place of prayerful contemplation where the Word of God speaks to the hearer from his or her heart. (See page 8 for further instruction.)

Guilt of the Nation (4)

John Henry Cardinal Newman spoke of two types of faith: notional faith and real faith. Notional faith involves people who claim to believe in God but exhibit no signs of their belief in daily life. Real faith is a belief influencing every aspect of a person's life. People with notional faith may easily become captured by the spirit of the world while neglecting the spirit of God. The priests in the Book of Hosea are examples of a notional faith about God, knowledge of God that has no impact on their life. They have nothing to teach the Israelites.

✠ *What can I learn from this passage?*

Upheaval in Israel (5:1–14)

When a company's leader retires, many of the workers who had difficulty with him or her celebrate the departure. Others in the company, however, may fear life will become more difficult under their new boss. They may speak an oft-heard saying: "The devil you get may be worse than the devil you have."

Judah needed help from the Assyrians and became a vassal of the king of Assyria, who drained Judah of its wealth. In times of turmoil, nations often formed foolish alliances, trusting in material strength while forgetting about the importance of the Lord and the power of prayer. In our current era, Pope Francis asked people throughout the world to pray and fast for peace. This is a powerful and safe weapon against an enemy.

✠ *What can I learn from this passage?*

PART 2: INDIVIDUAL STUDY (HOSEA 5:15—14)

Day 1: The Crimes of Israel (5:15—7)

Although the author makes no mention of a lion in the following passage, he links the passage with the previous passage in which the Lord is compared to a lion. Like a lion returning to its lair, the Lord will leave the people until they repent and seek the Lord, which will happen when they realize their need of the Lord in the midst of their suffering. The Lord struck them down, and the Lord will give them life again. The presumptuous Israelites believe the Lord will come after two days, raising them up on the third day. The days are not considered exact predictions of a period of time, but rather a period of devastation followed by a period of revival, like the coming of dawn or like a spring rain refreshing the earth.

The Lord, recognizing the fickleness of Ephraim and Judah, proclaims their loyalty to be as fading as the morning mist and dew that disappear early. Because of their fickleness, the warnings of punishment given by the prophets were fulfilled. The Lord desires loyalty and a living knowledge of God, not empty sacrifices and burnt offerings.

The Lord declares the Israelites violated the covenant at a place named Adam, which was close to the area where the Israelites crossed the Jordan when they entered the Promised Land (see Joshua 3:16). The places once used in the northern kingdom for the worship of the true God (Gilead and Shechem) are now places for evildoers, with the priests committing terrible crimes, waiting like bandits to murder the people on the road to Shechem. The Lord is witnessing the horrible prostitution defiling Ephraim (Israel). Besides the punishment in store for the northern kingdom of Israel, the Lord has also passed judgment on Judah.

In chapter 7, the Lord speaks of being prepared to restore the good fortunes of Israel and heal her wounds, but the Lord witnessed the falsehood, the thievery, and banditry of Ephraim and Samaria (another name used by Hosea in referring to Israel). The people seem to believe the Lord forgets their crimes, but their sins are all around them, in the sight of the Lord.

The Lord sees their wickedness that makes kings rejoice and princes act with treachery. In the period between the death of King Jeroboam II (743 BC) and the fall of Samaria (721 BC), nearly all the kings of Israel were murdered. Because of the treachery and murder of the kings and princes, the Lord speaks of them as adulterers who were like a blazing oven which the baker stops stoking after kneading the dough. A baker keeps the oven warm with the intention of helping the dough rise without baking the bread. When the baker decides to stoke it again, the fire in the oven is ready to again blaze up. Like this oven, the treachery of the people lingers and can blaze up at any time.

The Lord speaks of the princes becoming sick with poisoned wine "on the day of our king" (7:5). The expression "on the day of our king" appears to refer to the inauguration feast of the king. The poisoned wine drunk by the princes points to the treachery in their plans to kill the king. During the night, their anger is subdued by sleep, but in the morning it flares up again like an oven, and they consume (kill) their rulers.

The Lord states the people of Ephraim align themselves with other nations, an action that includes aligning themselves with the gods of other nations. Ephraim becomes as worthless as an unturned cake, which is burned on one side and not cooked on the other. The foreign nations have consumed the power of the people of Ephraim, who take no notice of it. In their pride, they do not turn back to the Lord.

The people of Israel are like a silly and senseless dove that is easily captured. Instead of trusting the Lord, they seek help from Egypt and pay tribute to Assyria. The Lord will bring them down in a net like the birds of the air and punish them when they assemble. Because they rebelled against the Lord, ruin will come upon them.

Although the Lord wished to redeem them, they told lies about the Lord, saying the Lord abandoned them and refusing to plead with the Lord when they were in anguish. When they worshiped idols, they consumed the wheat and wine offered to them and ritually lacerated themselves with the hope of gaining a good harvest from the idols. Despite the training and strength they received from the Lord, they plotted evil against the Lord and became as useless as a defective bow. Because they refused to learn the language of the Egyptians, the Egyptians will ridicule them.

Lectio Divina

Spend 8 to 10 minutes in silent contemplation of the following passage:

The kings of Israel turned to false gods. In time, they were cheating and killing. Some of them became king by killing the previous king. Their life became a good example of the ripple effect of sin. Once they accept sin in their life, other sins often follow. In worshiping idols, the kings of Israel turned against the Lord, forgetting all the Lord had done for them. Although the author of Hosea speaks of the Lord punishing the people, the reality is the people punished themselves by sinning and causing grief and hardship for others. All nations that forget about the Lord or worship a false image of a vengeful and unloving God seem to cause great pain for the world and themselves, even today.

✠ *What can I learn from this passage?*

Day 2: From Glory to Corruption (8—9)

The Lord urges the people to sound the alarm, a trumpet blast warning the inhabitants the Assyrian army is soaring over the house of Israel like an eagle as punishment for discarding the covenant and rebelling against the law of the Lord. Although the people stress their familiarity with the Lord, they actually reject the Lord, placing themselves at the mercy of the enemy. The people of Israel chose kings and princes, but without the authority or knowledge (permission) of the Lord. Because they sinned by using their silver and gold to shape idols for themselves, they will experience devastation.

The Lord rejected worship of the image of the calf, introduced by King Jeroboam I in Samaria (Israel) after the separation of Israel from the southern kingdom of Judah. The Lord's anger will turn against them. He will ask how long they will be incapable of innocence. Artisans have made the image of the calf, which is no god and which will be shattered. Their worship of the calf will be like sowing in the wind, which the Lord will make a whirlwind of punishment on the people. Like wheat having no heads, the Israelites shall be useless. Even if the people of Israel were to flourish, their enemies will devour them, and they will be as worthless as useless vessels. They sought help from Assyria like a wandering wild ass, bargaining for lovers (supporters in battle). When they seek the help of other nations, the kings and princes of these nations will crush them.

In making many altars, which the Israelites believed would rid them of their sins, they were actually building altars to idols, thus sinning. Although the Lord in the past decreed laws for them, they became strangers to the Lord, loving to sacrifice meat and eat it, but the Lord is not pleased with their sacrifices. The Lord will punish their sinfulness and return them to Egypt, the land from which Moses led them. Israel ignored the Lord and built forbidden palaces. Judah also built fortified cities, and the Lord will send fire upon them and devour their fortifications. The Babylonians would set Judah ablaze during the invasion of the land.

In chapter 9, the Lord warns Israel not to rejoice like other nations. They have prostituted themselves, abandoning the Lord, enjoying a prostitute's fee on every threshing floor. Since the threshing took place at the time of harvest, the image of the threshing floor appears to be an allusion to a harvesting festival in honor of Baal. The Lord declares the wine from the harvest will not nourish them.

The people of Ephraim will no longer dwell in the land given them by the Lord, but some will return to Egypt and others will be brought to Assyria where they will eat unclean food. They will not pour out libations to the Lord and their sacrifices will not please the Lord. In exile, they will eat mourners' bread, the food eaten at funerals, making those who eat it unclean. Mourners' bread was considered unclean because anything eaten in the presence of a corpse was unclean. The forbidden food will be for those sinners who are hungry for it, but it cannot be brought into the house of the Lord.

The Lord asks what they would do on the festival day of the Lord, an apparent reference to the Israelite autumnal feast of Booths. When they flee from the devastation of the Lord, Egypt will receive them and Memphis will bury them. Memphis, known for its grand tombs, is in Egypt. The desolation will become evident as weeds grow over their silver treasures and thorns cover their tents.

The days of punishment and repayment will come upon them. They will call the prophet a fool and a madman, refusing to listen to him. The prophet is a watchman of Ephraim, yet the trap is all around, ready to ensnare him. Since the people of Ephraim have sunk into the depths of corruption, the Lord will punish them for their iniquity.

The Lord recalls the era when Israel was like grapes in the desert because of the protection of the Lord. The Lord protected their ancestors like the first fruits of a fig tree. When they came to the place called Baal-peor, they consecrated themselves to the Shameful One (Baal) and became as abhorrent as the thing they desired. Baal-peor was where the Israelites consecrated themselves for the first time to Baal. Ephraim is like a bird, whose glory flies away and who is no longer able to conceive or give birth. Even if they have children, the Lord will destroy them until no one survives. The Lord declares, at one time Ephraim was like a tree that had been planted in a meadow, and now the children of Ephraim will be slaughtered. The Lord will give them a womb which will miscarry and breasts which are dry.

The Lord rejected the people of Ephraim at Gilgal, a place where they practiced idolatry. Because of their wickedness, they will be driven out of the Lord's house. The Lord will reject their rebellious leaders and no longer love the people. The root of Ephraim is dried up, unable to bear fruit. Even if they were to bear children, the Lord will slay them. Because they refused to listen to the Lord, the Lord will disown them and make them "wanderers among the nations" (9:17).

Lectio Divina

Spend 8 to 10 minutes in silent contemplation of the following passage:

The people of the northern kingdom of Israel need the help of the Lord, and they cry out they know the Lord, but in reality, they do not know the Lord. They are familiar with the Lord, but their knowledge of the Lord does not keep them from worshiping false gods. True knowledge of the Lord demands more than rubbing shoulders with the Lord. It demands living and worshiping as the Lord wishes and avoiding the worship of false idols such as greed, illicit pleasure, and the many other temptations we experience in life.

✠ *What can I learn from this passage?*

___

Day 3: Punishment of Israel's Wickedness (10)

Israel is like an abundant vine covered with fruit. The more plentiful its fruit, the more altars it built, and the more productive the land, the more sacred pillars it constructed. Sacred pillars were established for worship, very often for the worship of false gods, although the Israelites set up sacred pillars in honor of the Lord of Israel when they first entered the Promised Land. At the time Hosea wrote this book, the people of Israel were unfaithful to the Lord and were building altars and pillars to false gods. Because the Israelites abandoned faith in the Lord, the Lord will smash their altars and sacred pillars.

In the desolation arising from the corruption of Israel and the power of the Assyrians invading the land, the people proclaim they have no king, a sign the king is too politically weak to fulfill his duties, or a sign no king sits on the throne. The Lord is the real king of Israel, but the people lack both respect for the Lord and the faith to trust the Lord can help them. The people make empty promises, swear false oaths, and enter into sinful covenants. Lawsuits arise like poisonous weeds, indicating that the power to administer justice no longer exists.

The inhabitants of Samaria (Israel) and the priests of the false gods mourn over the calf of Beth-aven, an idol taken to Assyria as an offering to the king of Assyria. Since many of the idols were covered with gold, silver, and other forms of jewelry, nations often confiscated the precious idols of the conquered nations. Assyria's capture of the calf brought shame to the people of Israel who, without faith in the God of the Israelites, are left stranded.

Israel and its king will disappear like a twig in water and the places of idol worship, where the Israelites sinned, will be destroyed, their altars overrun with thorns and thistles. The destruction refers to the Assyrian subjugation of Israel which was to take place in 721 BC. The devastation of the land will be so horrible the people will cry out to the mountains and hills to crumble and cover them.

The Lord declares Israel has sinned since the days of Gibeah, a place where the tribes of Israel sinned by fighting among themselves (see Judges 20). The Lord chastises the people of Israel by inciting other nations against them in payment for two crimes, which were not identified.

The Lord pictures the early days of Ephraim, portraying it as a trained young cow which had not yet given birth, enjoying the work of threshing the wheat. The Lord "laid a yoke upon her beautiful neck" (10:11), signaling the power of the Lord over the people. All the tribes of the Israelites worked on the land, planting justice, and reaping loyalty. They prepared a new field and sought the Lord who would come and rain justice on them.

Unfortunately, Ephraim plowed evil, harvested wickedness, and ate the fruit of falsehood. Because the people of Israel trusted their own power and army, the Lord foretells a time when war will break out and all their fortresses will be destroyed. Hosea writes about a battle involving Salman, who ravaged Beth-arbel. Just as this bloody battle involved killing mothers and children, so it will happen for Bethel because of the wickedness of the people. At dawn, the king of Israel will disappear. Dawn was usually depicted in the Bible as a time pointing to a renewal by the Lord, but in this passage, it becomes a prediction of a new and tragic period for the people of Israel.

Lectio Divina

Spend 8 to 10 minutes in silent contemplation of the following passage:

During the Depression, many wealthy people lost most of their money after the stock market crashed. As a result, a number of them, whose aim in life centered on gaining wealth, committed suicide. They made their wealth their god, and when their god was lost, they lost all incentive for living.

Similarly, the people of Israel had abandoned the God of Israel and set their hearts on worshiping an idol representing Baal. When the Assyrians took their idol from them, they had no one left to worship.

Jesus foresaw the human tendency of making wealth a god and he wisely warns us to establish for ourselves a lasting treasure. He realized people put a great deal of energy into their heart's desire, whether that desire be wealth, popularity, or some other form of personal gain. He tells us to set our hearts on storing up treasures in heaven, adding, "For where your treasure is, there also will your heart be" (Matthew 6:21). No one can take that treasure from us.

✠ *What can I learn from this passage?*

Day 4: A Parent for Israel (11—12)

Hosea portrays the Lord as a parent speaking of Israel as a child, a reference to the era when the Lord led the Israelites out of Egypt. The Lord often called them, but the more the Lord called, the farther away they went, sacrificing to the Baals and burning incense to idols. Like a loving parent, the Lord taught the people of Ephraim how to walk in the Lord's presence.

Although they were taken into the loving arms of the Lord, the people of Ephraim did not understand how much the Lord cared for them. The Lord drew them lovingly to himself, "with bands of love" (11:4). In a previous passage, the Lord put a yoke on the people, but here the Lord leads them with a band of love, an expression which connotes a more gentle approach to leading the people. Continuing to use the image of a loving parent, the Lord speaks of caring for the people like those who lift children to their cheeks and who bend down to feed them.

Unfortunately, the people of Ephraim rejected the Lord, who must now become a punishing parent. Since the people refuse to repent of their wickedness, the Lord will return the people back to Egypt and will place others under the rule of Assyria. The sword will destroy the diviners of the false gods and devour the people because of their devious ways. The Lord's people have chosen apostasy by denying the Lord and worshiping false gods. Even if the people call out to the God of Israel with one voice, the Lord will not lift them up from their desolation.

After this warning, the Lord relents, asking how the God of Israel, like a parent, could deliver up Israel and treat the people like those who live

---

in Admah or Zeboiim. Admah and Zeboiim were cities near Sodom and Gomorrah who shared in the destruction of those two cities.

Unable to remain angry with the people, the Lord takes pity on Ephraim, declaring Ephraim will not be destroyed again. When the Lord speaks of Ephraim in this passage, the reference is to the people of Ephraim who fled from Israel when the Assyrians invaded.

Since the Lord is God, the Holy One, and not a human being, the Lord will not act in a human manner, seeking revenge. When the Lord roars like a lion over the land, the children of God will come full of fear and trembling like birds and doves from Assyria, from the west and from Egypt. The Lord will resettle the people of Israel in their homes. Many of the people of the northern tribe of Israel fled to Judah and Israelite colonies in Egypt at the time of the Assyrian invasion. At the end of the Babylonian exile, the Lord directed the Israelites to return and settle in Judah as a unified nation, which included those from the northern kingdom of Israel and those from the southern kingdom of Judah.

In chapter 12, the Lord contrasts the faithfulness of Judah with the deceit of Ephraim. Listing some of the infidelities of Ephraim, the Lord declares Ephraim has become a deceitful nation, negotiating with other nations and accepting their gods. Judah, on the other hand, has remained faithful to the Lord and to the "holy ones," a reference to the subordinate lower gods of the divine council. Ephraim sinned by making a covenant with Assyria and Egypt instead of trusting in the Lord.

Hosea, speaking the Lord's message, reverses some incidents found in the Book of Genesis to convey the message of this chapter, which is a message of infidelity on the part of Israel and Judah. The Lord has a disagreement with the Israelites, referred to in this passage under the name of Jacob. An angel of the Lord changed Jacob's name to Israel (see Genesis 32:23–29). The Lord will repay Jacob for his devious conduct, meaning a punishment for all Israelites. The passage refers to the birth of Jacob. Esau, Jacob's twin, was born first and had the right to the inheritance, but Jacob was born clutching the heel of Esau. In Hosea, the Lord claims Jacob supplanted his brother, even in the womb (see Genesis 25:21–26). Jacob will later deceive his blind father, Isaac, who mistakenly blesses

Jacob as his heir rather than Esau, the firstborn (see Genesis 27:1–45).

As a grown man, Jacob wrestled with an angel all night and prevailed (see Genesis 32:23–31). Jacob wept and entreated the angel, a reference to his pleading prayer. Jacob then declared he saw God face to face and lived. At Bethel, Jacob vows, "the LORD will be my God" (Genesis 28:21). Since Hosea is viewing Jacob in a negative manner, deserving of punishment, he could be implying Jacob's vow was insincere or simply another trick. In Hosea, the Lord states Jacob (the Israelites) must return to the God of their ancestors, living with loyalty, faithfulness, and hope in the Lord.

The Lord compares Ephraim to a cheating merchant who holds a false balance in his hands, extorting wealth from the people and bragging how rich he has become. The Lord declares his riches shall not purchase forgiveness for sin. Hosea notes the Lord claimed to be the God of the Israelites from the time they left Egypt, and the Lord now predicts they will again live in tents as they do when celebrating the feast of Booths. For seven days, the Jewish people live in tents (booths) to commemorate the time the Israelites lived in tents in the desert.

Throughout the ages, the Lord continued to speak to the people through the prophets who received visions and parables. Since the people did not listen to the prophets, their words came to nothing.

The Israelites would construct a mound of stone as a sacred pillar and a sign of a covenant between people. The Lord declares the signs of covenants of peace were stones placed in a mound to represent a sacred pillar. The Lord protests they are falsehoods, just a heap of stones which mean nothing. The Lord continued to send prophets to Israel. After deceiving his father, Isaac, into giving him the blessing, Jacob had to flee to Aram where he became a servant tending sheep for the sake of receiving a wife (see Genesis 28:5, 29:15–30, 30:31). The story of Jacob and his sons eventually leads the whole nation to settle in Egypt. Through Moses, who is considered a prophet, the Lord brought Israel out of the slavery of Egypt and tended the people.

Hosea abruptly adds that Ephraim aroused the anger of the Lord who cast blood guilt on him to repay him for his guilt. This passage lays the groundwork for the next chapter.

Lectio Divina

Spend 8 to 10 minutes in silent contemplation of the following passage:

A common experience for many parents is the rebellion of a child or children, usually during their teenage years. The parents love them, but when their children reject the authority and love of the parents, parents find themselves confused and helpless.

The God of Israel has the same experience with Judah and Israel, the Lord's special children. Just as many parents realize they lost control of their children and must allow them to suffer their own consequences, so the Lord does the same with the Israelites. History, in fact, shows the Lord does the same with all of creation. The Lord loves us and wants us to respond with love and obedience. We are left with the choice of accepting or rejecting God's love for us.

✠ *What can I learn from this passage?*

Day 5: Sin and New Life (13—14)

Since this chapter consists of several oracles of the Lord placed together, it sometimes becomes confusing whether the Lord is speaking of a specific tribe of Israel or of all the people of Israel.

The Lord speaks of Ephraim as the strongest of the northern tribes, with an exalted position among the tribes of the northern kingdom of Israel, but Ephraim brought spiritual death to itself by worshiping Baal. Although Hosea often referred to all of Israel when speaking of Ephraim, he here refers to the tribe of Ephraim in contrast to the other tribes of the northern kingdom. Ephraim worships idols made by artisans, offers sacrifices to the idols, and follows the ritual of kissing the molten calf. Because of the sins of the people of Ephraim, they will pass away like a morning cloud, the dew, chaff from the threshing floor, or smoke out of a window. The Lord reminds them that ever since they left Egypt, the Lord has been their God, their own savior, unlike the gods they do not know.

Hosea now includes all of Israel in the following oracle. Although the Lord satisfied the hunger and thirst of the Israelites in the desert by providing for their needs, they became proud and forgot the Lord. As a result, the Lord pledges to become like a lion, a leopard, or a bear to "tear their hearts from their breasts" (13:8). Like a wild animal, a lion, the Lord shall rip them open and devour them.

The Lord taunts Israel, asking where is their new king who will rescue them when the Lord destroys them. They wanted kings and princes to lead them, so the Lord in a rage gave them kings and took them away in anger. The giving and taking of kings and princes may be a reference to the line of kings of Israel who were killed one after another. The Lord compares Israel to an unwise child who refuses to be born when the time comes and chooses instead to remain in the womb of their wickedness. When the time comes for birth and the child refuses to leave the womb, the mother and the child die. The Lord will condemn Ephraim to death (Sheol), asking if they expect the Lord to redeem them when they choose to remain in their sin and not come to birth by returning to the Lord. Lacking compassion for these sinful people, the Lord will call upon the plague and sting of death to come upon the people.

Hosea returns to speaking about Ephraim as a specific tribe in Israel. Although Ephraim shall flourish and be exalted among his brother tribes, an east wind (Assyria) will come from the Lord to consume the land, the water, and the treasure of the people. Thus, chapter 14 begins with Samaria (Israel), guilty of rebelling against the Lord, destroyed, their children smashed to pieces and their pregnant women ripped open. If Ephraim cannot withstand the onslaught of the Assyrians, the rest of Israel will certainly succumb.

Hosea becomes the one who speaks in 14:2, calling the people to return to the Lord, their God, reminding them of their downfall due to their sinfulness. When they return to the Lord, they are to beg the Lord to forgive their wickedness and to offer the Lord what is good, not an offering of first fruits, but an offering of the fruit of their lips, their words. They know neither an alliance with Assyria nor the power of horses will save them. Idols will not help them, but the Lord alone, who has compassion for the orphan, will help them.

The Lord responds to the people's pleas, promising to heal their apostasy, love them freely, and abandon all anger against them. The Lord will bring new life, like dew for Israel who will blossom like a lily. Israel will become as fertile as the cedars of Lebanon, and its shoots will reach out. Israel's splendor shall be like the olive tree and its fragrance like the cedars of Lebanon. The people will live in the shade of Israel, raising grain, blossoming like the vine, and becoming as well known as the wine of Lebanon. The Lord has humbled Ephraim and rejected his idols, and the Lord will now be to them "like a verdant cypress tree" and provide fruit for the people.

In a short epilogue, Hosea asks who is wise enough to understand these things, stating a lesson learned from this book, namely the paths of the Lord in which the just walk are straight, while sinners stumble.

Lectio Divina

Spend 8 to 10 minutes in silent contemplation of the following passage:

> In the Book of Hosea, the prophet is teaching us the need for patience in trusting the Lord and not making the material goods of the world our gods. Wisdom tells us not to ignore the needs of our daily life, but it also tells us to make the Lord a living presence in all the decisions of our life. An underlying message is to trust the love of God, to pray, and to live our life as people faithful to the Lord. As Hosea says, "Straight are the paths of the LORD" (14:10).

✠ *What can I learn from this passage?*

Review Questions

1. How does Hosea apply the image of Ephraim being like an "unturned cake" (7:8)?
2. Why did the Lord grow angry when Ephraim sought help from other nations like Assyria and Egypt?
3. What does Hosea say about the Lord's concern for the people and their response (see 9:10)?
4. What does the image of the Lord as a parent tell us about the anguish of the Lord concerning Ephraim?

LESSON 3

The Books of Joel and Amos

It shall come to pass I will pour out my spirit upon all flesh. Your sons and daughters will prophesy, your old men will dream dreams, your young men will see visions (Joel 3:1).

Opening Prayer (SEE PAGE 15)

Context

Part 1: Joel 1—2 The Book of Joel consists of two speeches. Joel prophesied after the Jews returned from exile, somewhere between 450 and 350 BC. He is familiar with the Temple built in Jerusalem before the Babylonians destroyed it and exhibits knowledge of Temple liturgy. During his lifetime, the Jews had no king. He prophesies at a time when locusts devoured the land that was already devastated, badly in need of rain for the new crops. He warns about devastation coming at the hands of the Lord and calls upon the people to turn back to the Lord. The Book of Joel speaks positively about the day of the Lord, the final Judgment Day, which will bring blessings upon the Israelites.

Part 2: Joel 3—4 and Amos In the last two chapters of the Book of Joel, the Lord promises to bring the people of Judah to a secure end. The spirit of the Lord will be poured out on all the people of Judah, and the Lord will punish the nations opposing Judah.

The Book of Amos begins with a series of oracles of the Lord against nations oppressing the northern kingdom of Israel. In three speeches, the Lord calls upon the people to take note of the warnings of destruction in store for those who refuse to listen to the Lord's word. The Lord then speaks of three woes afflicting those who ignored the covenant and perform useless sacrifices to empty idols. Amos experiences five visions concerning the destruction of Israel and warns the people about the punishment about to be inflicted on them for their mistreatment of the destitute. In the end, the Lord will bless Israel with abundance.

PART 1: GROUP STUDY (JOEL 1—2)

Read aloud Joel 1—2.

1 Total Disaster

Joel addresses the elders and all the people who endured a dry winter and a land ravaged by a swarm of locusts. The prophet questions whether anyone ever experienced anything like this before or even heard about such a thing from their ancestors. He tells the people they should instruct their children about the devastation and direct them to pass the news on to their children's children.

Joel refers to the invasion of the locusts under four different names, calling them the cutter, the swarming locust, the hopper, and the consuming locust. The four titles may refer to different species of locusts or some phase in the locust's maturing process.

Joel calls upon the drunkards and all those who love wine to wake up and wail over the new wine taken from them. The imagery of waking up refers to the inaction of the people who apparently are accepting their plight with complacency, as though it were a passing occurrence. They do not think of attributing the locusts' onslaught as coming from the Lord. Without grapes on the vine for making wine, the drunkards and wine lovers would especially bear the burden of the loss. In telling them to wake up, Joel is expressing a sense of urgency.

Joel pictures the locusts as a numerous, powerful army, an army with teeth like a lion and lioness, stripping the forest bare and sheering the bark off trees, leaving only white branches exposed. He urges the people to wail like a young woman dressed in sackcloth, grieving over the death of her husband to whom she was betrothed. Although the marriage ceremony did not take place yet, the people of Joel's era considered the man and woman as belonging to each other as though they were husband and wife. In the absence of grain offerings and libations needed for Temple worship, the priests and ministers of the Temple are especially in mourning. Joel's concern for the worship and the Temple becomes evident from his emphasis on the inability to make offerings for worship.

Joel speaks of the farmland as though it were a person. Without grain, grapes for wine, and crops for oil, the devastated farmland mourns. Because the vines, the wheat, the harvest in the field, the fig tree, the pomegranate, the palm tree, and every tree in the field have dried up, the farmers and vine dressers join the land in mourning and cry out to the Lord. The land is dry and parched, not only from the locusts but also from the lack of winter rain. Just as the land dried up, so, the prophet tells us, the joy of the people dried up along with it.

Joel summons the priests and ministers of the altar to lament, pressing them to spend the night in sackcloth. Ordinarily, priests prayed from sunrise to sundown. Joel's request, asking the priests to spend the night in sackcloth, points to the urgency of always praying for help. Joel again stresses the news about the house of the Lord lacking grain offerings and libations needed for worship. He rallies the priests to assemble the people and the elders in the house of the Lord so all may plead with the Lord.

Joel warns the people the Day of Judgment, or the day of the Lord, is imminent, coming as a day of destruction from the Lord. The Day of Judgment in the Scriptures may be presented as a day of destruction or a day of joy. Joel attempts to convince the people the judgment they are enduring is a result of their sinfulness. The depletion of the food supply leads to grieving in the house of the Lord. The sadness experienced in the Temple is a reference to the Temple festivals, days when the people assembled in joy to offer their grain and animal offerings to the Lord.

Because of the desolation of the land and the lack of rain, seeds shrivel in the parched dirt, the storehouses are empty, the granaries are in disrepair, animals groan, the cattle suffer from a lack of pasture, and the sheep are starving. In the fields, the fire has devoured the pastures and scorched all the trees. In the midst of this suffering, Joel, along with the wild animals, cries out to the Lord for help.

2 A New Beginning

In an attempt to motivate the people to pray, Joel pictures the swarming onslaught of locusts as an army led by the Lord. The alarm is sounded in Zion on the day the Lord comes, causing fear and panic among the inhabitants. The swarming locusts come to Zion like a day of darkness and gloom, a day of thick clouds. The imagery points to a militia of locusts swarming over the land and covering it with the darkness of their presence. They move steadily, like the light of dawn crawling over the mountains. Joel declares nothing like this ever happened before and nothing like it will happen in the distant future. The devastation moves along like fire, devouring everything, leaving behind a scorched land. Before the army arrives, the land looks as glorious as Eden, but behind it the land becomes a desolate, ravaged wilderness.

Joel describes the swarm as looking like warhorses, galloping over the land, thundering like the rumble of chariots across the mountaintops. They sound like the crackling of flames, demolishing everything and marching like an army in battle formation. The people's faces turn pale in fear. The swarm rushes along like warriors, moving straight ahead and never breaking rank. They plunge unchecked through the weapons of the people, scale the walls, and clamber into houses. They enter through windows like thieves. As they darken the sun, moon, and stars, the earth trembles and the heavens shake. At the head of the army is heard the voice of the Lord. The army is immense and obedient to the Lord's voice. Joel wonders who could survive such a terrifying day.

In answer to Joel's call for prayer, the Lord responds with a sudden reversal of the catastrophe. The Lord calls the people to return to their God, the God of Israel, with their whole heart—fasting, weeping, and mourning. They are to rend their hearts instead of their garments, returning to the gracious and merciful Lord who is slow to anger, abounding in unwavering love, and relenting in punishment. Joel implores the people, saying the Lord may relent and bless them with grain offerings and libations necessary for worshiping the Lord. The promise of a blessing of grain and libations for worship stresses Joel's concern for Temple worship.

Joel calls the people to sound the alarm, proclaim a fast, gather together, and sanctify the assembly. They are to gather together the elderly, the children, even infants. The bridegroom should leave his room and the bride her bridal tent. Between the porch and the altar, the place where the people meet the priests and offer sacrifice, the people and the ministers are to weep before the Lord, begging the Lord to spare them and not bring the Lord's heritage to a shameful end, which would make them a disgrace among the nations. Nations would say, "Where is their God?"

The prayer of the people leads the Lord to relent and act with compassion. Joel announces the news the Lord is sending grain, new wine, and oil to satisfy the ravaged inhabitants. Besides these gifts, the Lord promises never again to shame the people before the nations. Although locusts do not come from the north, the Lord refers to them as "the northerners" and promises to drive them out to a dry, empty land, littering the shores of the Dead Sea, referred to in Joel as the "eastern sea," and the shores of the Mediterranean, referred to as the "western sea." The odor of dead locusts will be sickening.

Joel instructs the people not to fear but to rejoice in the splendid deeds of the Lord. He tells the wild animals in need of vegetation not to fear because green grass will return. Informing the people of Zion the trees will bear fruit, the fig tree will produce figs, and vine will produce a great harvest, he rallies them to rejoice in the Lord their God, who will grant them the early and late rains as in the past. The sign of their prosperity will be threshing floors full of grain and vats gushing over with new wine and oil. The Lord will repay twofold what the Lord's army of swarming locusts, the hopper, the consuming locusts, and the cutter have eaten.

The Lord proclaims the people will eat until they are fully satisfied and will praise the name of the Lord for the wonderful concern shown them.

The Lord promises they will never again experience shame. The people will know the Lord, their God, beside whom there is no other.

Review Questions

1. How does Joel describe the invasion by the locusts?
2. Why is Joel so concerned about the lack of offerings for worship?
3. What leads the Lord to relent and avoid punishing the people?

Closing Prayer (SEE PAGE 15)

Pray the closing prayer now or after *lectio divina*.

Lectio Divina (SEE PAGE 8)

Relax your body and maintain a posture of prayer (back straight, eyes shut, feet flat on the floor). This exercise can take as long as you want, but in the context of this Bible study, 10 to 20 minutes should be sufficient.

The meditations that follow are provided only to help group participants use this prayer form, but note that lectio is intended to bring one to a place of prayerful contemplation where the Word of God speaks to the hearer from his or her heart. (See page 8 for further instruction.)

Total Disaster (1)

A man went to a hospital to visit a friend whose neck was broken in an automobile accident. Because he wore a brace, the friend could look neither to the right nor to the left. The man told his friend he was praying for him, but the friend commented he did not believe prayer would help. The friend said, "What happens, happens, and we can do nothing about it." As much as the man protested to his friend that prayer would help, the friend remained stubborn and refused to believe God had time to care for him.

Joel witnesses the devastation of the land and calls the people to pray to God for help. He knows some of the people will refuse to respond to his call, saying, like the patient with the broken neck, "What happens, happens, and we can do nothing about it." Many people think this way when they encounter a seeming impossibility in their life, but Jesus has

---

a different point of view. He tells us to knock and the door will open for us. When we pray, something happens. God never says no. Perhaps the answer to our prayer is not exactly what we ask for or perhaps we never see it, but it is something good because God loves us. God may not give us what we ask for, but God will answer with what we need.

✠ *What can I learn from this passage?*

A New Beginning (2)

Suffering is inevitable in life. What is important is our response to it. The people of Joel's era were suffering from an onslaught of an army of locusts devouring everything in their land, leaving the people with nothing to eat or drink. Joel rallied them to pray as a unified nation. Prayer was their response to suffering, and the Lord heard their prayer, bringing them early and late rain to provide an abundant harvest of grain, wine, and oil. Trusting the Lord and offering our suffering as a prayer is a powerful plea for God's blessings. A pastor once told his people that he wondered whether people would pray if there were no suffering in life.

✠ *What can I learn from this passage?*

PART 2: INDIVIDUAL STUDY (JOEL 3—4, AMOS)

Day 1: The Day of the Lord (Joel 3—4)

In the Acts of the Apostles, the author describes Peter as preaching his first sermon to the people after the descent of the Holy Spirit in the form of tongues of fire on Pentecost (see Acts 2:14–41). In his speech, Peter paraphrases the entire third chapter of Joel and sees its fulfillment in Jesus' mission.

This chapter speaks of some period in the future when the spirit of the Lord will be poured out on all people, leading their sons and daughters to prophesy, their old men to dream dreams, their young men to see visions, and their male and female slaves to receive the spirit. The gift of prophecy would no longer be reserved to a few, but many will receive this charism. Joel could view this gift as a fulfillment of Moses' words: "If only all the people of the LORD were prophets! If only the LORD would bestow his spirit on them!" (Numbers 11:29).

Joel describes the day of the Lord as a cataclysmic event, with signs in the heavens, the sun turning dark and the moon blood red, and signs on earth, with blood, fire, and columns of smoke. In the Book of Exodus, the Lord performed miracles in the heavens and on earth. When Aaron, the brother of Moses, touched the Nile, it turned to blood (see Exodus 7:20), and the Lord led the people by means of a column of cloud by day and a column of fire by night (see Exodus 13:21). In this passage from Joel, the prophet is describing a new Exodus leading to salvation. These cataclysmic events will take place before the great and terrible (awesome) day of the Lord. On that day, those who call on the name of the Lord will be saved. As predicted by the Lord, a remnant will be surviving on Mount Zion. Among the survivors in Jerusalem will be the ones specially called by the Lord.

In chapter 4, the Lord speaks of restoring the good fortune of Judah and Jerusalem. In those days, when this happens, the Lord will gather all the nations, bringing them into the Valley of Jehoshaphat. The name Jehoshaphat means "the Lord judges," a symbolic name used to designate the punishment Judah's enemies will receive. Because of their sins against Judah, the Lord will judge them, accusing them of scattering the people of Judah, dividing up the land, trading boys for prostitution and young girls for wine.

The Lord confronts Tyre, Sidon, and all the regions in Philistia, asking if they are paying the Lord back for something. The image of paying the Lord back for something reflects the thinking of the era that often viewed people punished in the same manner they punished others. Since the nations lacked the ability to punish the Lord, the Lord will punish Tyre, Sidon, and the regions in Philistia with a punishment equal to their crimes. Just as these nations seized the silver and gold belonging to the Lord, bringing them to their temples, and sold the Lord's people to the Greeks, sending them far from their homeland, so the Lord will sell their sons and daughters to Judahites (the original inhabitants of Jerusalem), who will send them far away to the Sabeans, traders from the southwestern tip of the Arabian peninsula.

The Lord instructs Joel to proclaim a holy war and alert the soldiers to prepare to march into battle by beating their plowshares into swords and their pruning knives into spears. Even the weakest will become a warrior. The Lord bids all the neighboring nations to battle with the Judahites. They are to come to the Valley of Jehoshaphat, the Valley of Judgment, where the Lord will judge them.

Using agricultural images to describe the battle, the Lord directs the people of Judah to wield the sickle to cut down the enemy, depicted as a ripe harvest. They are to tread the wine press to overflowing with the abundant crimes of their neighbors. The image of the wine press was occasionally used to refer to the blood of the enemy. Large numbers of the enemy descend into the Valley of Decision, another name for the Valley of Jehoshaphat. The sun, moon, and stars are darkened, indicating the day of the Lord, the Day of Judgment, is near. The Lord roars like a lion from Zion and Jerusalem. Although the heavens and earth quake, the Lord will be a shelter for the Lord's people.

When all this happens, the people will know the Lord is truly the God of Israel who dwells on Zion, the Lord's holy mountain. The Lord proclaims Jerusalem will be holy and strangers will never pass through her. On that day, the mountains will flow with an abundance of new wine and milk, and all the streams of Judah will flow with water. From the house of the Lord, a spring will rise to water the ordinarily arid Valley of Shittim, southeast of Jerusalem.

The Lord declares Egypt and Edom will become a wasteland because these nations shed the innocent blood of the remnant of Judah. Despite the violence done against Judah, the Lord promises Judah and Jerusalem will be inhabited forever.

Lectio Divina

Spend 8 to 10 minutes in silent contemplation of the following passage:

> On Pentecost, the Spirit of the Lord brought courage to Peter, who immediately began to preach about Jesus, using a prophecy from Joel for his message (see Acts 2:16–21). The Spirit of the Lord not only touched the heart of Peter but also touched the heart of those listening to him so they were able to understand Peter's message and seek baptism. Whenever someone speaks about Jesus, the spirit of the Lord is active in the speaker and the hearer. In Joel, the Lord promised to pour out the spirit upon all flesh. In Peter's message at Pentecost and its favorable reception by the people, we find an example of the Spirit of the Lord at work in the hearts of the listeners.

✠ *What can I learn from this passage?*

Day 2: Oracles Against the Nations (Amos 1—2)

Amos was a sheep breeder from a town in Judah named Tekoa. He received a vision when Uzziah was king of Judah and Jeroboam II was king of Israel, and two years after an earthquake so devastating people still remembered it. The Lord roars like a lion from Zion, making the fertile pastures of the shepherds languish and the summit of Mount Carmel, in the northwest corner of Israel, wither. Amos, who lives in the southern kingdom of Judah, is sent by the Lord to the northern kingdom.

The first two chapters in the Book of Amos consist of oracles against nations that were once aligned with or subject to the idealized Israelite kingdom of David and Solomon. These nations should have dealt faithfully with the Israelites as well as with one another, but they rebelled instead. They once belonged to the Lord, and the Lord will not take them back. The oracles are against the cities within these nations.

Amos' first oracle is against Damascus, a capital of Syria. The expression "for three crimes…, and now four," which is repeated in each oracle, is an expression of the Lord's frustration in dealing with nations. In other words, "Enough is enough." The Lord has had enough of the crimes of Damascus

(Syria). Syria threshed the people of Gilead, a town in Israel, destroying the city like a thresher crushing grain with its iron shafts. The Lord will destroy the cities and rulers of Syria, sending devastating fire on the house of the ruler, Hazael, the strongholds of Ben-hadad, and the barred gate of Damascus. The Lord will dethrone their ruler from the Valley of Aven (valley of wickedness), and the people of Aram will be exiled to Kir, which was the place where the Assyrians used to exile their prisoners.

The Lord's next oracle is against cities in Philistia. For three crimes and now four, the Lord will refuse to take Gaza back. Because the people exiled an entire population to Edom, the Lord will demolish their wall and strongholds with fire and cut down their king from Ashdod and Ashkelon, cities linked with the Philistines. The Lord's hand will turn against Ekron "and the last of the Philistines shall perish" (1:8).

The Lord speaks an oracle against Tyre. For the three crimes of Tyre and now four, the Lord will not take them back. They handed over an entire population of Israel to Edom and rejected the covenant they made with the Israelites. The Lord will send fire on the wall of Tyre and devour its stronghold.

For the three crimes of Edom and now four, the Lord will not take it back. Edom (descendants of Esau) pursued his brother with the sword, showing no compassion but instead raging in endless fury. The Lord will send fire on Teman and devour the strongholds of Bozrah, two cities of Edom.

For the three crimes of the Ammonites and now four, the Lord will not take them back. In order to extend their territory, they ripped open the pregnant women of Gilead. The Lord will cast fire on the wall of Rabbah (Amman) and devour its strongholds. In the midst of battle and tempest, their king shall go into exile along with his princes, says the Lord.

For the three crimes of Moab and now four, the Lord will not take it back. In retaliation for burning the bones of Edom's king to ashes, the Lord will send fire upon the nation and devour the strongholds of Kerioth. Since many people of ancient times believed the burning of a person's bones to ashes forced the spirit of the dead to roam around with nowhere to find a peaceful rest, it was considered a monstrous crime. Moab will die amid the tumult of battle cries and ram's horn, the horn which sounded the battle cry. The Lord will slay the ruler and all the princes with him.

For the three crimes of Judah and now four, the Lord will not take it back. Because the people rejected the instruction of the Lord, disobeyed the Lord's statutes, and followed their ancestors' lies by worshiping the false gods who led them astray, the Lord will set fire on Judah and devour the strongholds of Jerusalem.

For the three crimes of Israel and now four, the Lord will not take them back. Up to this point, the people of the northern kingdom of Israel would applaud the Lord's judgment on the nations, but they would never have expected this indictment against themselves. Commentators believe this oracle is the pinnacle of all that went before.

The Lord lists a number of crimes attributed to the people of Israel. They sell the just for silver and the poor for a pair of sandals; they trample into the dust the heads of the destitute, and kick the lowly out of their way; son and father force themselves on the same girl, thus profaning the name of the Lord; the rich sin by reclining beside the altar on the cloaks of the indebted poor without giving them back when evening arrives. Although the poor would often give their cloak as a pledge in return for a loan, the Book of Exodus protects the poor by decreeing the cloak must be returned before evening (see Exodus 22:25). The rich sin even more gravely by drinking wine in the Temple purchased at the Temple's expense for the sake of worship.

The Lord recalls all that was done for the Israelites. The Lord destroyed the Amorites who appeared to the Israelites to be as tall as cedars and as strong as oak trees and destroyed their fruit and their roots. The Lord brought the Israelites up from Egypt and led them through the desert for forty years to their occupation of the land of the Amorites. The Lord raised up prophets among them and Nazirites among their young men, facts which the Lord challenges them to deny. A Nazirite was a consecrated man who pronounced vows and refrained from drinking wine. Because the people made the Nazirites drink wine and ordered the prophets not to prophesy, the Lord grieves and groans under the burden of their wickedness like an animal pulling a wagon laden with sheaves.

As punishment for the people of Israel, the swift shall not run fast enough, the strong will become weak, the warrior will be killed, and the archer cut down. The fastest runners and those on horses shall not save their life. The most valiant of warriors shall flee naked in disgrace on that day, says the Lord.

Lectio Divina

Spend 8 to 10 minutes in silent contemplation of the following passage:

Although the prophet speaks of the Lord punishing the people, the people actually punish each other. Nations break their alliances with each other and engage in war, thus destroying each other. Some of the people in Israel, who believed in the Lord, sinned against their neighbor by causing the poor to lose their freedom, dignity, or life just for the sake of their own more luxurious and pleasure-filled life. Injustice, greed, and selfishness reach far back into history.

✠ *What can I learn from this passage?*

Day 3: A Threefold Summons to Hear the Word of the Lord (Amos 3—5:6, 8)

Amos speaks the Word of the Lord, the first of three summonses addressed to the whole family of the Israelites whose ancestors were brought out from Egypt at the time of the Exodus. The Lord chose only the family of the Israelites among all the nations of the earth. However, because of the Israelites' intimate knowledge of the Lord, the Lord will punish them more severely for their offenses. In a series of rhetorical questions, the Lord challenges the people to reflect on the favors given to them. The Lord asks if two would go on a trip together without agreeing to do so. The implication is the Lord and the Israelites both agreed through a covenant to journey together.

Amos, in chapter 3, continues to list a series of questions from the Lord, proving the Lord has a purpose in sending a message to them through a prophet. "Does a lion roar in the forest when it has no prey," or does a young lion cry out from its den unless it has captured something? Does a bird swoop down on a trap on the ground unless there is something to lure it? "Does a snare spring up from the ground without catching anything?" Does the ram's horn, which is blown at a time of attack, sound in the city without the people becoming frightened? Does disaster come upon a city without the Lord causing it? An addition to the text, sounding like a commentary by an editor, states the Lord God does nothing without revealing the plan to the prophets, the servants of the Lord.

After asking the previous questions, the Lord asks who would not fear when the lion roars. When the Lord God has spoken, "who would not prophesy?" The Lord instructs the prophets to proclaim the Word of the Lord in the strongholds of Assyria and Egypt. In doing this, the Lord is inviting the nations who once oppressed Israel to gather on the mount of Samaria (Israel) and witness the great turmoil and oppression within it. The people of Israel have no intention to do what is right, says the Lord.

Israel is storing up violence and destruction in their strongholds. Although the Lord sends other prophets to speak out against the people of Israel for worshiping false gods, the Lord's words to Amos emphasize the injustice of the people against each other. The Lord predicts an enemy shall surround the land, tear down the fortresses, and pillage the strongholds of Israel. Just as a shepherd rescues only a pair of sheep's legs or the tip of an ear from the lion's mouth, so shall the people of Israel escape "with the corner of a couch or a piece of a cot" (3:12).

The Lord speaks an oracle against the house of Jacob (Israel). On the day the Lord punishes Israel for its crimes, the Lord will also punish the altar of Bethel, causing the horns of the altar to break off and fall to the ground. The Lord will destroy the luxurious life of the people. Their rich winter and summer homes, made of ivory, shall lie in ruins with their abundant rooms in shambles, says the Lord.

In chapter 4, a second summons is addressed to the women of Samaria. The Lord addresses them with an extreme form of insult by calling them cows of Bashan. Bashan is a fertile area east of the Sea of Galilee where fat herds of cows grazed. The women along with the men oppress and abuse those who are destitute and needy. The women call out to their husbands to bring them a drink, a symbol of their arrogance and indifference to others.

The Lord swears days are coming when they will drag the women away with ropes and their children with fishhooks. It was a custom of the day to put fishhooks through the cheeks of the people to keep them together as they staggered into exile. The captives will go out through the breaches in the walls, walking in single file, and will be exiled to Harmon, apparently a place in the northern part of Israel already under the control of Assyria.

The Lord sarcastically tells the people they might as well go to Bethel and Gilgal where they worship false gods and where they bring their sacrifices each morning and offer their tithing every third day. The Lord invites them to burn leavened bread as their thanksgiving sacrifice and proclaim openly their voluntary offerings. The Lord seems to be saying, "Since they are sinning, they might as well allow their sins to increase." Punishment is inevitable.

The reason the Lord afflicted the people was based on the hope they would realize they were being punished for their sinfulness and would repent. Although the Lord punished the people by depriving them of food and bread in all their cities, the people refused to return to the Lord. The Lord punished them by withholding rain from them at planting time and by sending rain on one city or one field and not on another. People would travel to the cities having water, but the water was never adequate enough to satisfy them. Despite the lack of water, the people still did not return to the Lord. The Lord sent blight and mildew, locusts to devour their gardens and vineyards, and caterpillars to consume their fig and olive trees, but the people refused to return to the Lord. The Lord then sent a disease like the one the people suffered in Egypt. The Lord sent armies to kill their young men, capture their horses, and fill their camp with the stench of the dead, but the people did not return to the Lord. Finally, the Lord destroyed some of them just as the Lord destroyed Sodom and Gomorrah, leaving the living like a brand snatched from the fire, yet they did not return to the Lord.

Since the people did not repent, the Lord warns the people to prepare for the worst from the mighty Lord who forms mountains, creates winds, reveals the thoughts of the people, makes dawn fade into darkness, treads on the heights of the earth, and whose name is the Lord, the God of hosts.

Amos, in chapter 5, continues to bring the Word of the Lord to the people of the northern kingdom of Israel. The Lord grieves over virgin Israel, which has fallen, never more to rise. After the Assyrian invasion of the kingdom of Israel, the names of the northern tribes of Israel disappeared from the earth and the land of Israel was abandoned with no one to help the survivors. The Lord God speaks of disaster for Israel, declaring a city, marching out with a thousand, shall return with a hundred, and another, marching out with a hundred, shall return with ten.

Amos brings a message of hope to the people of Israel, telling them to seek the Lord so they will live and to abandon the false gods of Bethel, Gilgal, or Beer-sheba, the places where many of the Israelites worshiped idols. The Lord declares the people of Gilgal and Bethel shall be led into exile and oblivion. If the people of Israel do not repent, the Lord's anger will flare up like fire against the house of Joseph (Israel) and consume Israel in an unquenchable fire. The reference to the "house of Joseph" is a reference to the main tribes of Israel, the tribes of Ephraim and Manasseh, which descended from Joseph, one of the twelve sons of Jacob.

Amos declares the true Lord is the one who made the constellations (Pleiades and Orion), who brings the dawn and the night, who summons the waters of the sea and pours them out on the land, and who brings sudden destruction on the stronghold and fortress. The Lord created and controls all of creation and is able to destroy the wicked, no matter how powerful and protected they may be.

(Note: The verse numbers in 5:1–9 in the latest version of the *New American Bible* are rearranged to follow the proper sequence of original manuscripts. After verse 6, the Bible lists verses 8 and 9 in this section. Verse 7 properly belongs to the first of the three "woes" that follow.)

Lectio Divina

Spend 8 to 10 minutes in silent contemplation of the following passage:

History has many lessons of empires that grew powerful, but because of greed, selfishness, pride, excessive sensuality, or disregard for the poor and needy, they collapsed. Israel and Judah were once powerful nations, but they rejected the precepts of the Lord and the Israelites fell into the hands of their invaders. The fall of the invincible Roman Empire in the fifth century shocked many people of that era. Reading the history of the Israelites and the fall of great empires in history, we must wonder how long any nation can exist without remaining faithful to the Lord.

✠ *What can I learn from this passage?*

Day 4: Three Woes (Amos 5:7, Verse 10 to Chapter 6)

Amos speaks of the Lord casting words of "woe" on those who reject justice and trample down honesty. They turn justice into something bitter, like the taste of wormwood. They hate those who accuse them at the meetings at the gate, and they despise those who speak the truth. Judgments in ancient times took place in the square near the gate of a city, with the elders of the people acting as judges. Amos brings a warning from the Lord. Because the judges tax the poor and extort unfair levies for their grain, they shall not live in their fine houses of hewn stone and they shall not drink their wine, despite their fine vineyards. The Lord is aware of their many crimes and sins of oppressing the poor, which include accepting bribes for a favorable judgment and rejecting the needy at the gate, the place where many of the poor would sit and beg. Accepting bribes in compensation for a lenient judgment was explicitly forbidden by the Lord (see Numbers 35:31–32). Amos or an editor inserts a confusing proverb which states "the wise are struck dumb for it is an evil time" (5:13).

Amos has a message for the judges. The Lord exhorts them to seek goodness, not evil. If they do, the Lord, the God of hosts, will have compassion on the remnant of Joseph remaining in Israel. If they choose evil, lamentations will be heard in every square and street. They will call upon the farmers and mourners to wail and lament over the withering vineyards as the Lord of judgment passes through. In the Book of Exodus, the Lord speaks of passing through the land of Egypt and striking down every firstborn of the men and the beasts (see Exodus 12:12). As a result of this passage of the Lord, a loud wailing was heard throughout Egypt (see Exodus 12:30). Wailing was a common reaction to grief in ancient times.

Casting a second "woe" on the people of Israel, the Lord addresses those awaiting the day of the Lord, the Judgment Day. The day of the Lord will be a day of darkness, not a day of light as some suspect, but a day without hope. Those who flee from the lion will encounter a bear, and those entering a dark house and leaning against a wall will be bitten by a snake. The day of the Lord will be a dark day of overwhelming hopelessness.

Because of the injustice practiced by the people, the Lord rejects their feasts and festivities. They may engage in the external rituals of the law, but the Lord will refuse to accept their burnt offerings and their grain and communion offerings. The Lord will not listen to their strident songs or the melodies of their harps. Instead, the Lord seeks justice surging like waters and honesty flowing like a constant stream.

Using the experience of the Israelites in the desert, the Lord stresses the people's faithfulness to the Lord is more important than their sacrifices. The Israelites, who traveled through the desert for forty years, did not offer sacrifices or incense, yet the Lord protected them. The lack of animals and grain for offerings in the desert did not deter the Lord from guiding them. Amos expresses the displeasure of the Lord, who predicts the people will carry false idols of the Assyrian gods (Sukuth and Kaiwan) into exile with them, beyond Damascus, far from their homeland.

In chapter 6 of Amos, the Lord casts a third woe on Jerusalem and Israel, telling them to look to the cities of Calneh, Hamath, and Gath, which were destroyed by the Assyrians in the eighth century BC. The Lord asks if Jerusalem or Israel were any better or larger than these. The Lord views the Israelites as living in denial concerning the day of disaster and hastening their coming destruction by their violent crimes. They live in luxury, lying in lavish beds made of ivory and lounging on their couches, composing music on the harp like David, drinking wine from bowls, anointing themselves with the finest oils, and unconcerned about the collapse of Joseph (Israel). Because of their manner of life, their revelry shall cease and they shall be the first to go into exile. A conquering army ordinarily led off the important people of the conquered territory first.

Because the Lord despises the pride of Jacob (Israel) and his fortifications, the Lord will turn over the city and all in it to the invaders. If a single house remains with ten people in it, they shall all die. When a relative or someone who prepares the bodies for burial picks up the remains to carry them out of the house and someone in the house should ask if anyone is with him, he shall answer that no one is with him. The reference is not clear. It may refer to a plague which often follows a battle. Although someone must prepare the body for burial, others would avoid the corpse, afraid of being infected. When the man says no one is with him, others in the house are to remain silent and not speak the name of the Lord. This could result from a superstition based on the belief the Lord has punished them, as though the Lord may hear them and become enraged.

Amos continues to speak of the punishment from the Lord. The Lord has already given the command to the enemy to smash the majestic houses and totally destroy the small houses. Just as a horse cannot run over rock or one cannot plow the sea with oxen, so the people will receive punishment because they have forced justice and righteousness to become for them as bitter as gall or wormwood. When King Jeroboam II of Israel was fighting against Judah, Israel recaptured two of its cities (Lodebar and Karnaim), giving the kingdom a false feeling of invincibility. The reality is the Lord is raising up a nation to oppress the whole land of the Israelites, the land once included as the boundaries of the kingdom of Solomon.

Lectio Divina

Spend 8 to 10 minutes in silent contemplation of the following passage:

The rich people of Israel received many gifts from the Lord, but they used them for their own luxury and power while cheating the poor to gain more for themselves. The Lord was willing to forgive them, but they refused to forgive those under them. The Lord eventually turned these unjust stewards over to the tortures of the invading armies. The selfish people of Israel had no compassion for the needs of others. The message teaches us the Lord, who has forgiven our sins, also gives us many gifts so we may serve others and not for the sake of enabling us to feel more important than others.

✠ *What can I learn from this passage?*

Day 5: Symbolic Visions (7—9)

Chapters 7—9 speak of five visions received by Amos. In the first vision, the Lord was preparing a swarm of locusts to attack when the late growth began to grow. The late growth referred to the growth after the "king's mowing," a reference to the practice of paying the first growth to the king as a tax. The people needed the late growth to survive. When Amos begs the Lord to forgive Israel, who is so helpless and small before the Lord, the Lord relents and declares this devastation from the swarm of locusts shall not take place.

In the second vision, the Lord summons a rain of fire which would devour the depths and the fields. Amos begs the Lord not to destroy the people, asking who will be able to raise up Israel (Jacob) who is so small and helpless. The Lord relents, declaring the destruction would not take place.

In the third vision, the Lord was standing by a wall built with the help of a plummet, a tool. A plummet was used to measure how far a wall or a building was out of line to determine if it had to be torn down. When the Lord asks Amos what he sees, Amos answers that he sees a plummet. The Lord plans to lay the plummet in the midst of the people of Israel, apparently to show how far out of line they have grown and how they deserved to be torn apart. The Lord refuses to forgive them any longer. Along with the people, the places of worship in Israel shall be destroyed, the sanctuaries made desolate, and the family of Jeroboam killed. Unlike the first two visions, Amos does not beg the Lord to relent.

Amaziah, a priest of Bethel, sent word to Jeroboam that Amos' words were demoralizing the people and Amos was conspiring against him (Jeroboam) by saying Jeroboam would be killed by the sword and Israel will definitely be forced into exile. Believing Amos belongs to a group of professional prophets who prophesied for payment, Amaziah exhorts Amos to leave Bethel, the Lord's sanctuary, and to earn his bread by prophesying in his homeland of Judah. Amos defends himself, saying he is not a prophet, nor does he belong to "a company of prophets." He states he is a herdsman (sheep breeder) and dresser of sycamore trees whom the Lord took away from his flock with the mission of prophesying to the people of Israel. Because Amaziah demanded he leave Israel, Amos has dire words for him and for all the people of Israel. He declares Amaziah's wife shall become a prostitute, his sons and daughters shall be killed by the sword, his land will be taken from him, and he will die in an unclean land, a land deprived of the ritual cleanliness demanded by Israelite law. He adds that Israel will be exiled from its own land.

Chapter 8 describes a fourth vision, in which the Lord shows Amos a basket of end-of-summer fruit. The Lord asks Amos what he sees, and Amos declares he sees a basket of end-of-summer fruit. In the next sentence, the Lord declares the end has come for the people of Israel, playing on the word "end," and making the end-of-summer fruit refer to the end of the nation of Israel. The Lord will forgive the Israelites no longer, causing the Temple singers, who ordinarily sing joyful songs to the Lord, to wail. Corpses shall be strewn everywhere. The people again call for silence in a superstitious fear that calling on the name of the Lord will doom them.

The Lord addresses a message to those who tread on the destitute and enslave the poor people of Israel. The cheating merchants ask when the new moon will be over, a reference to the end of the religious festivals during which merchants could not sell their grain. They also anxiously ask when the Sabbath will end so they can sell their grain. When they do sell their goods, they intend to diminish the ephah, which means they will cut back on the amount of grain they claim to sell to the buyer and they will add to the shekel, meaning they will charge more for the grain than they should. They will also fix their scales so they can cheat their customers.

Besides cheating their customers, the merchants will also buy the poor for silver or a pair of sandals. In the days of Amos, people sold their freedom to survive, indebting themselves to the merchants. Besides these evil acts, the merchants will cheat the poor by selling them worthless grain.

Amos prophesies, saying the Lord, who swears by the name of Jacob, the father of Israel, will not disregard what the rich have done. The land and all who dwell in it shall tremble in fear, tossed around like the Nile which floods annually and later subsides as the river does in Egypt. The Lord will make the sun set at midday, covering the light of day with darkness. This appears to be a reference to a solar eclipse, which the ancients viewed as an ominous sign of future danger. Mourning shall darken the land, festivals and songs shall become dirges, loins shall be covered with sackcloth, every head shall be shaved bald, people shall mourn as though for the loss of an only child, and weep on as on a day of bitterness.

The Lord pledges to send a famine on the people, not a famine marked by a desire for food or drink, but one of longing to hear the Word of the Lord. The people became accustomed to the Lord using prophets to speak to them, but the Lord now refuses to send prophets, leaving the people longing for the Lord to speak to them through the prophets. In the Book of 1 Samuel, we read of the time when Samuel was a young man and the Word of the Lord was rare and visions uncommon (see 1 Samuel 3:1). When prophets were rare among the Israelites, the people became uneasy.

Amos prophesies the people of Israel shall wander over the whole land, from sea to sea and from north to east, searching for the Word of the Lord, but they shall not find it. Beautiful young women and men will faint from thirst. Those who swear by the goddess Ashima in Samaria and worship a false god from Dan to Beer-sheba will fall, never rising again. The area from Dan to Beer-sheba is a reference to the whole land of Israel.

The final chapter of Amos relates a fifth vision. Amos sees the Lord standing beside an altar, apparently an altar at Bethel, which was once the place of worship for the people of Israel and later used as a place for idol worship. The Lord speaks of striking the pinnacles so the threshold shakes, crashing down on the people. The scene could allude to an earthquake or the massive destruction brought by the enemy. Those who remain after the devastation will be killed with the sword, leaving no one to escape. The people believed the Lord could not reach into Sheol, the place of the dead, but the Lord declares that even if people were to dig down to Sheol to hide, the hand of the Lord will destroy them.

Amos declares the Lord will hunt them down and destroy those who climb to the heavens on the highest mountains or hide on Carmel's summit. On Mount Carmel, there were many caves and crevices for hiding. No matter where they go, the people cannot escape the wrath of the Lord. Even if they attempt to hide from the Lord's gaze at the bottom of the sea, the Lord will command the serpent to bite them. The reference to the serpent, the monster of the deep in mythology, is not clear in this passage, except to say no matter where the people go, they will not be safe from the Lord. The Lord will destroy with the sword all who go into captivity.

Amos speaks of the glory of the Lord. The Lord, the God of hosts, whose touch melts the earth, who built the upper chamber in heaven, whose vault is established over the earth, who summons the waters of the sea and pours them out on the surface of the earth, is truly the Lord. Although the Lord loves Israel, the Lord also shows concern for all nations, pointing to the Ethiopians, the Philistines, and the Arameans whom the Lord helped in the past. It is the same concern the Lord showed for the Israelites who were led by Moses from the land of Egypt.

The Lord is always watching the sinful kingdom of Israel, soon to be erased from the face of the earth. Pledging not to destroy the nation of Israel completely, the Lord plans to sift the people out like a sifter who refuses to let something as small as a pebble fall to the ground. The sinners shall be killed by the sword, many of whom foolishly believe the Lord will not destroy them because they belong to the people of God.

An epilogue added to the Book of Amos appears to be a later addition, apparently written after the return of the Israelites from exile. The addition follows the tradition of ending a book on a more positive note, explaining how the Lord will rebuild and restore the land and the spirit of the people. The book ends with words of encouragement for Israel. The Lord will raise up the house of David, meaning the Lord will establish a king for the people. As a sign of the renewal of the people, the Lord will fill in the breaches in the wall, restore the ruins, and rebuild the nation. The people shall acquire the remnant of Edom and of all the nations belonging to the Lord.

The days are coming when those who plow and plant will overcome those who reap the harvest, and the vintager will overtake the sower of the seed. The crops will be so abundant the time of harvest will hardly end before the time of planting begins. The days of prosperity will come as the mountains drip and run with the juice of grapes. The Lord will restore Israel, guiding the people in rebuilding and inhabiting their ruined cities. On that day, they will plant vineyards, drink the wine, plant the gardens and eat its abundant fruit. The Lord will plant them on their own ground, never again to be plucked from the land the Lord gave them.

Lectio Divina

Spend 8 to 10 minutes in silent contemplation of the following passage:

> Jesus told a parable about separating lambs from sheep, meaning separating the good from those who were evil. Jesus tells the good they will inherit the kingdom of heaven. On the other hand, Jesus tells the evil people to depart from him. He tells them he was hungry, thirsty, a stranger, naked, ill, and in prison, and they did not care for him. He ends by saying, "What you did not do for one of these least ones, you did not do for me" (Matthew 25:45).

> When the Lord instructed Amos to speak to the people, Amos warned them against cheating, enslaving, or abusing those who were destitute. Those who hurt the poor and needy were condemned by the Lord. Just as Jesus identified with the poor and destitute in the Gospels, so also the Lord identified with the needy in the Book of Amos. The way we treat others is the way we treat the Lord.

✠ *What can I learn from this passage?*

Review Questions

1. What does Joel mean by "the day of the Lord?"
2. Why does the Lord pronounce an oracle against the nations in chapters 1 and 2 of the Book of Amos?
3. What is the Lord's major concern in each of the three summonses?
4. What is the Lord's concern in each woe cast upon the people?

LESSON 4

The Books of
Jonah, Obadiah, and Micah

In days to come the mount of the LORD's house shall be established as the highest mountain; it shall be raised above the hills, and peoples shall stream to it (Micah 4:1).

Opening Prayer (SEE PAGE 15)

Context

Part 1: Jonah The story of Jonah differs from the other prophetic writings insofar as it is not a collection of oracles from the Lord passed on by the prophet, but a story which is at times humorous, sarcastic, and ironic in its presentation. It centers on the actions and misdeeds of a disobedient and reluctant prophet of the Lord. The fascinating story reads like a parable or fable with a message appearing to have its source in stories and legends told about a prophet who lived long before the story unfolds.

Although it is difficult to determine when the author wrote this story, it appears to have been written after the exile. In the story, the Lord chooses Jonah to go to Nineveh to preach to the people, but Jonah goes in the opposite direction, away from Nineveh. Nineveh is the capital of the empire of the Assyrians which caused a great deal of suffering for the people of Judah during the eighth century before Christ.

In an attempt to escape from the Lord, Jonah finds himself in the midst of a storm and must admit to the frightened sailors he is fleeing from the Lord. The sailors throw Jonah over the side of the ship where a large fish swallows him and eventually deposits him on dry land. Jonah preaches in Nineveh and the people repent. The story conveys a message about the Lord's concern for all people, not just the Israelites.

Part 2: Obadiah, Micah The Book of Obadiah, which in the canonical order of the Bible actually appears before the Book of Jonah, is the shortest book of the minor prophets. It centers on the Israelites' relationship with Edom (descendants of Esau). After the Babylonians invaded Judah and exiled many of its inhabitants, Edom took advantage of the weak condition of those remaining in Jerusalem and invaded Judah. The book depicts the Lord's retaliation toward Edom and the blessings bestowed on Mount Zion (Jerusalem). An unknown author penned the Book of Obadiah.

The Book of Micah consists of a collection of speeches and proclamations attributed to the prophet Micah, who lived during the time of first Isaiah, before the Babylonian invasion of Jerusalem in 587 BC. Like Isaiah, Micah is familiar with God's choice of the Israelites as the Chosen People, but he refuses to accept the notion that such a special call guarantees the city's security. Portions of the book, like some of the other prophetic books, were heavily edited by later writers. Micah focuses its attention on Judah as it existed under the threat of the Babylonian invasion. It speaks of the impending invasion and the exile the people of Judah will endure as a punishment from the Lord, but it guarantees salvation will follow. The Lord will pass judgment on the sinfulness of the people of Judah and will end with a positive note concerning God's forgiveness of the people.

PART 1: GROUP STUDY (JONAH)

Read aloud the Book of Jonah.

1 Jonah's Disobedience and Flight

The Word of the Lord came to Jonah, the son of a man named Amittai, who lived during the reign of Jeroboam II (786–746 BC). The naming of Jonah as the son of Amittai does not mean Jonah actually existed, but it could be the author's way of adding some authenticity to the story. Aware of the wickedness of the people of Nineveh, the Lord directed Jonah to go to the great city of Nineveh and preach against it. "Great" will be used fourteen times in the story, stressing the use of embellishments in the story.

Jonah, a true Israelite, hated the Assyrians for the destruction they caused the Israelites, and he immediately made plans to flee westward to Tarshish, away from the Lord and far from Nineveh. At Joppa, he found a ship headed for Tarshish, paid the fare, and set to sea with the crew. The Lord, however, sent a great wind upon the sea, causing a storm so great that the ship was about to break up. Each of the frightened sailors cried out to each of their gods, and they sought to lighten the ship to keep it afloat. Apparently, Jonah slept through the storm while the crew members threw their cargo into the sea. The astonished captain found Jonah and asked why he was asleep. He ordered Jonah to get up and pray to his god, hoping Jonah's god would not allow them to perish. The irony of the story is that Jonah could sleep through the storm, trusting the crew, while he did not trust the Lord.

The crew, believing one of them caused the gods to become angry, decided to cast lots to discover who was responsible for bringing this evil upon them. The guilty lot fell to Jonah. They demanded Jonah tell them why they were enduring this evil, asking him to speak about himself, what was his business, where did he come from, and to what country and people did he belong. Jonah answered he was a Hebrew who fears "the God of heaven, who made the sea and the dry land" (1:9).

When the crew heard Jonah's story, a great fear seized them, and they questioned how he could do such a thing. They asked Jonah what they should do with him for the sea to calm down. Since the crew members, not knowing Jonah's God, did not know whether killing him would enkindle the wrath of his God, Jonah himself offered the solution. The sea was growing more angry. Jonah instructed them to hurl him into the sea, predicting the sea will then become calm. Jonah confessed the storm came as a result of his flight from the Lord. The irony of the story shows the back-and-forth trust Jonah has in the Lord. Earlier, lacking a desire to respond to the Lord's command, he proclaimed his trust in the Lord's ability to calm the storm.

The story presents the crew in a compassionate manner. They decided to row harder to return to dry land rather than throw Jonah into the sea. When the storm grew more terrifying, the crew prayed to the Lord not to allow them to perish for taking the life of this innocent man. The story portrays the crew as prophetic in the sense they are the ones who recognized the need to fulfill the Lord's will concerning Jonah's mission.

They hurled Jonah into the sea and the storm ceased. Overcome with great fear of the Lord, the men sacrificed to the Lord and made vows to the God of the Hebrews. The story is one of conversion for the members of the crew, who previously worshiped their own gods.

2 Jonah's Prayer

The story becomes even more exaggerated as "the LORD sent a great fish to swallow Jonah," who remained in the belly of the fish for three days and three nights (2:1). Popular stories about Jonah in our modern era speak of the large fish as a whale, but the story itself says nothing about the particular type of fish. Understandably, however, readers of this story connected the description of a large fish in their imagination with that of a whale, hence the embellishment.

Jonah's prayer to the Lord from the belly of the fish allowed the author to present a message about our relationship with the Lord. The prayer, written as a psalm, seems to be an independent addition to the story at a later date. Some parts of the prayer do, however, fit the story line.

Jonah prayed, saying he called on the Lord in the time of his distress and the Lord answered him. He cried from the womb of Sheol, which is his way of saying he was near death (Sheol). He prayed directly to the Lord and said the Lord heard his voice. In his prayer, he noted the Lord cast him into the heart of the sea and the waters engulfed him with all its fury. In the belly of the large fish, he realized the Lord saved him from drowning.

In grief over the idea the Lord would no longer look on him with compassion, he wondered how he would ever again look upon the Lord's Temple. He prayed about the waters engulfing him up to his neck and the deep recesses of the sea enveloping him, wrapping seaweed around his head. He spoke about sinking to the roots of the mountains of the deep, being imprisoned in the bars of death, and he praised the Lord for raising him up.

In the past, when he was weak, he remembered the Lord and recalled the prayers he offered in the Lord's holy Temple. Those who worshiped worthless idols abandoned all hope for mercy, but Jonah, as one who worshiped the God of the Israelites, continued to hope in the Lord, offering sacrifices to the Lord. What he vowed to the Lord, he will do. Just as the sailors in chapter 1 vowed to the Lord, so Jonah in his prayer made a vow to the Lord. He recognized his deliverance was from the Lord. The Lord then ordered the fish to vomit Jonah up on dry land.

3—4 The Repentance of the Ninevites

The Lord again commanded Jonah to travel to the great city of Nineveh and announce the message the Lord will give him. Jonah obediently traveled to Nineveh, a breathtaking, large city that took three days to walk through. Jonah began his journey through the city, and when he had traveled only a single day announcing Nineveh would be conquered, the people of Nineveh believed the Word of the Lord and proclaimed a fast. All the people covered themselves with sackcloth, the clothing of repentance.

Upon hearing Jonah's message, Nineveh's king removed his royal garments, covered himself with sackcloth, and sat in ashes. Supported by the nobles, he decreed throughout Nineveh no person or beast, cattle or sheep shall eat or drink anything, adding all people and animals must be covered with sackcloth while pleading out loud to God. Hoping the Lord's wrath would cease and not destroy the city, he ordered the people to abandon their wicked and violent manner of life. Seeing how the people repented, the Lord relented and did not carry out the evil planned for the city.

In chapter 4, a disgruntled and angry Jonah prayed for the Lord to take his life. He knew the Lord, a gracious, merciful God, abounding in kindness, would save the people he (Jonah) hated so deeply. His hatred for the people of Nineveh had originally driven him to flee toward Tarshish. He became so depressed over the conversion of the people of Nineveh, he declared it would be better for him to die than live. The Lord responded to Jonah's sullen mood, asking if Jonah had the right to be angry.

Jonah left the city and built a hut east of the city to wait under it in the shade to see what would happen. Apparently, Jonah still hoped to witness the Lord's destruction of the city. To Jonah's delight, the Lord caused a wide-leafed plant to grow over his head, offering Jonah refreshing shade. The next morning, at dawn, the Lord sent a worm to attack the plant and caused it to wither. When the sun rose, the Lord sent a scorching east wind, and the sun beat so hot on Jonah's head he became faint. He again wished for death, saying it would be better for him to die than live.

God and Job entered into a confrontation, with the Lord asking Jonah if he had a right to be angry over the loss of the plant. Jonah responded, saying he had a right to be angry enough to die. The Lord chastised Jonah, berating him for his concern about a tree he neither planted nor caused to grow, a plant which grew up in one night and in one night perished. In contrast, the Lord had greater concern for the city of Nineveh with a population of more than 120,000 people who are ignorant of their unjust manner of life.

Review Questions

1. Why did Jonah and the Lord disagree concerning the preaching of the Lord's message to the Ninevites?
2. What theme do you find in the prayer of Jonah in the chapter 2?
3. What was the message of the plant that provided shade for Jonah?

Closing Prayer (SEE PAGE 15)

Pray the closing prayer now or after *lectio divina*.

Lectio Divina (SEE PAGE 8)

Relax your body and maintain a posture of prayer (back straight, eyes shut, feet flat on the floor). This exercise can take as long as you want, but in the context of this Bible study, 10 to 20 minutes should be sufficient.

The meditations that follow are provided only to help group participants use this prayer form, but note that lectio is intended to bring one to a place of prayerful contemplation where the Word of God speaks to the hearer from his or her heart. (See page 8 for further instruction.)

Jonah's Disobedience and Flight (1)

By sending Jonah to Nineveh, the Lord is showing love for all people, even those who were oppressing the Israelites. Jonah, the reluctant prophet, attempted to flee from the Lord, and the Lord chased after Jonah by using human means, namely a storm and a compassionate crew. The story's message is that the Lord has a mission for all people. No matter how much people attempt to flee from the Lord, the Lord goes after those people, using other people and events to draw them back to the fulfillment of the Lord's will.

✠ *What can I learn from this passage?*

Jonah's Prayer (2)

Jonah's prayer can resonate with people today who find themselves needing to trust God in difficult situations. Jonah speaks to the Lord about the waters engulfing him, dragging him down into the depths. When people in our modern world experience anxiety or worry, they sometimes feel themselves drowning in their problems and calling out to the Lord to rescue them from their situation. Jonah feels imprisoned, near death, with no hope of deliverance, yet he recognized the Lord helped him in his need. The message of the author of the story of Jonah is one of trust and hope in the Lord, who loves us.

✠ *What can I learn from this passage?*

The Repentance of the Ninevites (3—4)

In the story of Jonah, we encounter a similar type of story. Jonah remained loyal to the Lord, but he could not bring himself to act with the compassion and mercy shown by the Lord. In the world today, some people remain faithful to the rules of their faith without realizing the need to live with the love and forgiveness shown by the Lord. The Lord sought this love and forgiveness from Jonah and hopes to find it in all Christians.

✠ *What can I learn from this passage?*

PART 2: INDIVIDUAL STUDY (OBADIAH, MICAH)

Day 1: Edom and Judah (Obadiah)

The Edomites are descendants of Esau, the twin brother of Jacob and son of Isaac. Obadiah brings the message of the Lord to all the nations to go to war against Edom. The Lord pledges to make Edom the least among the nations. The people of the great city of Edom became arrogant and boastful, asking who could bring the country down to earth. During the time of the nation's grandeur, the people viewed the nation as a soaring eagle with its nests among the stars. The Lord pledges to bring it down.

Obadiah uses rhetorical questions to present the Lord's message. Would thieves steal until they had enough, or would grape pickers leave some of the grapes behind? The implied answer is "no." The treasures of Esau (Edom) shall be hunted down and their treasures taken. Those with whom Edom made covenants will join in driving out of its land the powerful nation of Edom. These deceiving allies, who ate bread with them, will replace the people of Edom with foreigners who lack knowledge.

The Edomites were noted for their wisdom. On the day the Lord sends armies against Edom, the wisdom of Edom will vanish and all the people on Mount Esau will be destroyed. The Edomites did nothing when strangers captured the wealth of Judah and cast lots for the treasures of Jerusalem, then Edom became like one of the invading strangers. When the Babylonians devastated Judah in 587 BC, the Edomites joined with them and captured the escaping people of Judah. After Jerusalem's destruction, the Edomites broadened their hold on Judah's southern territory.

Verses 12 to 14 sound as though they are speaking of a series of future warnings, but they should be read as having already taken place. The Lord informs the Edomites they should not have gloated over their brother, Judah, on the day of Judah's disaster. They should not have mocked the people of Judah on the day of their ruin or have spoken arrogantly on the day of Judah's anguish. When the people of Judah were suffering so grievously, they should not have entered the gate of the Lord's people with Judah's enemy. They should not have rejoiced over the misfortune of Judah on the day of Judah's tragic destruction or stood at the crossroads, killing the survivors of the invasion. On the day of Judah's distress, they should not have handed over the fugitives to the Babylonians.

The day of the Lord's judgment against all the nations is imminent. As these nations acted, so it will be done to them. Their conduct will be revisited on them. Just as they drank upon the Lord's mountain in defeating Judah, so will all the nations drink in defeating them. Nations will drink and swallow them, wiping them from the face of the earth, never to be heard of again.

Some of those on Mount Zion (Jerusalem) will escape and only later will the mountain again become holy. The family of Jacob will take back all those dispossessed from the land and living in exile. The house of Jacob (Judah) will be like a fire, the house of Joseph (Israel), a flame, and the house of Esau, stubble. The Israelites shall devour the house of Esau in flames, leaving no survivors.

The Israelites will take possession of the cities surrounding Judah and a major portion of the land of the Canaanites. The people of Judah, who delivered the land from the enemy, will ascend Mount Zion to rule Mount Esau. "The kingship shall be the LORD's" (1:21).

Lectio Divina

Spend 8 to 10 minutes in silent contemplation of the following passage:

> When Judah was at its weakest point, the people of Edom took advantage of the situation and conquered a portion of the land of Judah for themselves. Edom was later destroyed just as it destroyed portions of Judah, but unlike Judah, the entire nation of Edom disappeared from history. History can list nations, kings, rulers, and extremely wealthy people whose names were forgotten after they died. The last line of the Book of Obadiah sums up the last line of history, "...the kingship shall be the LORD's" (1:21). Jesus the Lord was born in a small town and preached in a small part of the world, and Jesus, the King of Kings, changed the whole direction of the history of the world.

✠ *What can I learn from this passage?*

Day 2: Oracles of Punishment (Micah 1—3)

The opening line of the Book of Micah identifies him as coming from Moresheth, a village in the Judean foothills, outside of Jerusalem. Micah prophesied under the kingships of three Judean kings, Jotham, Ahaz, and Hezekiah (around 759 to 687 BC). Micah declares he saw a message of the Lord concerning Samaria and Jerusalem, meaning it came to him in a vision.

Micah calls upon all the people to give strict attention to the message of the Lord which comes from the holy Temple as a witness against the people. The Lord leaves the Temple and treads on the high mountains of the earth, melting the mountains and splitting open the valleys, making the melted mountains flow like wax in a fire or water poured down a slope. The devastation sounds like a volcano erupting.

The devastation comes as a result of the sins of Jacob, the house of Israel in the northern kingdom. Micah asks what Jacob's crime is, and the answer is the sin committed in Samaria, most likely idolatry. Micah then asks what the sin of the house of Judah is, and the answer is Jerusalem, a reference to where some of the people worshiped false gods.

The Lord pledges to destroy Samaria (Israel), leaving it a devastated and cleared land, useful only for planting vineyards. The Lord will destroy the land with an invading foreign army, apparently the Assyrians in 722–721 BC. The stones of Samaria will fill the valley and lay bare the foundations of the city. All its carved figures will be shattered, its costly images burned in the fire, and all its idols destroyed. The wages of a prostitute, a reference to the offerings made to false gods, shall come to nothing.

Micah goes into mourning over the destruction of Jerusalem, lamenting and wailing, walking barefoot and naked, uttering sounds of lamentation like jackals, and mourning like the ostriches. The wound of the sin of Samaria is incurable and has reached even to Judah, to the gate of the Lord's people, even as far as Jerusalem. The prophet speaks of the devastation of a number of cities, many of them unidentifiable. He calls upon the people of the cities to mourn, making themselves as bald as vultures for the sake of the "children" whom they cherish. "Children" refers to the people of the cities who will be led into exile.

In chapter 2, Micah address the powerful people of Samaria as planners of evil who plot at night in their beds and carry out these deeds in the morning with no one powerful enough to stop them. They covet their neighbor's fields and seize them, and they cheat the people out of their homes and inheritance. These actions are abhorrent to the Lord. The First Book of Kings reports an incident about Naboth, an owner of a field, who refused to sell his field to King Ahab who coveted the field. Jezebel, Ahab's wife, had Naboth killed and Ahab took the land. As a result of the sin, the Lord sent Elisha to tell Ahab dogs will lick up his blood in the same place where the blood of Naboth was spilled (see 1 Kings 21:1–19). The punishment of Ahab indicates how much the Lord detests seizing the land of innocent people.

The Lord is planning evil against Israel which they cannot avoid. Because of their sinful lives, they will be humiliated and scorned. They will lament bitterly, totally ruined, with their fields divided among their captors who will not return them. They will have no one in the family of the Lord to allot a share of the land to them as happened when the Israelites entered the Promised Land and their leaders allotted the land to each of the tribes of Israel. Unhappy with the dire prophecies of Micah, the people rise up against him, warning him not to preach the things he is preaching. They refuse to believe they will be shamed as Micah predicts.

In response, Micah asks how the leaders of Israel can speak this way against the Lord, as though the Lord would become impatient for no reason. He is telling the people they have given the Lord a reason for punishing them. The Lord's word pledges good for those who are just. The powerful, however, act without justice. They refuse to listen to the Lord, acting against the people as though they were the enemy and stripping the garments from the peaceful and trusting, as if their garments were spoils of war. They expel the women from their pleasant homes and dispel forever the glory of the Lord from their children. Since the cast-out women have no one to defend them, the author may be implying widows are the ones cast out. Micah instructs the powerful leaders to depart because of their destructive uncleanness. They prefer a preacher who preaches lies about an abundance of wine and strong drink.

Micah then presents a more encouraging message from the Lord. When the Lord gathers the remnant of Israel like a flock of sheep or a herd of oxen into its pastures, the sound of rejoicing will erupt from the people (see Micah 2:12–13). The one who breaks through, meaning the Lord, will enter through the gate, and the king shall go through the gate before them with the Lord as their leader. Although the people view the Lord as their king, the passage appears to point to a future human king for the people.

Chapter 3 continues with Micah's bringing the Word of the Lord to the leaders of the Israelites, who are supposed to know what is right, but instead they hate good and love evil. The leaders are ravaging the people like cannibals tearing their skin from them, taking the flesh from their bones and eating it. Using images akin to preparing an animal for a meal, Micah claims the leaders skin the people, break their bones, and chop them to pieces like flesh in a kettle. When these evil rulers cry out to the Lord, the Lord will hide from them, refusing to answer their pleas because of all the evil they have committed.

Addressing the false prophets, the Lord accuses them of leading the people astray. They speak of peace, which the people want to hear, and receive food in return. When no one offers food, the false prophets speak of war. Because of their sins, they will receive darkness in place of visions and divination. The false prophets living in darkness will be disgraced and bewildered, remaining silent because the Lord does not speak to them.

Micah declares he is filled with the power of the spirit of the Lord, with the justice and might needed to declare to Israel the crimes and sins of the people. He calls the leaders of the house of Jacob, who abhor justice and misrepresent all that is right, to pay attention to the Word of the Lord. The leaders build up Zion with bloodshed and Jerusalem with wickedness, rendering judgment for a bribe, paying priests to pray, and disbursing fees to false prophets. They foolishly believe belonging to the family of Jacob will protect them from destruction. Because of these false leaders, "Zion shall be plowed like a field, and Jerusalem reduced to rubble" (3:12).

Lectio Divina

Spend 8 to 10 minutes in silent contemplation of the following passage:

Countries depend on just leaders to protect the rights of the people. Unfortunately, not all leaders are people of virtue. Without a faithful leader, a country can become a place of sin, filled with people who lie, cheat, kill, and steal.

Archbishop Oscar Romero lived in San Salvador when the government was oppressing the poor. The country's leaders trained their army to kill and oppress the common people. Romero dared to challenge the soldiers to have compassion for the people. In his last radio announcement before he was killed on March 24, 1980, he cried out to the soldiers, "I ask you, I beg you, I command you, stop the killing!" The soldiers were following the example of their military leaders, while Romero tried to lead them with an example of holiness and trust in God. The battle was not only one of the rich against the poor but also a battle of an unjust government against a great spiritual leader.

✠ *What can I learn from this passage?*

Day 3: Oracles of Salvation (Micah 4—5)

The tone of the Book of Micah changes from one of predictions about destruction to predictions about a glorious rebuilding of Jerusalem. The message in 4:1–3 is the same as that found in Isaiah 2:2–5. Although the passages are similar, almost word for word, it is not clear who originally penned these words. Did Micah borrow from Isaiah, or did Isaiah borrow from Micah, or did they both have another source that an editor incorporated into the books? Whatever the origin of the passage, both books speak of a glorious day for Jerusalem.

In 4:1–3, Micah declares the highest mountain shall be the mountain of the Lord's house. The Lord's house refers to the Temple, and the highest mountain refers to Jerusalem, which is not the highest material mountain as Micah claims. Micah is referring to the spiritual realm, not to the actual mountain of Zion. The passage views Jerusalem as perched above the world, seeing all and being seen by all. Nations shall stream toward this mountain, and people shall climb the mountain to the Lord's house, which means they will choose to worship the Lord of Israel, the God of Jacob, in the Temple.

Since Jerusalem knows the Lord, instruction in the ways of the Lord shall come from the people of Jerusalem to other nations. The message from the Lord shall be a message of a time of peace, a time when people will make implements of war, such as swords and spears, into implements for gardening (plowshares and pruning hooks). Wars will cease. Once people accept the God of Israel as Lord over all, they will come before the Lord on the holy mountain to settle their disputes in peace rather than in war.

In 4:4, Micah continues to speak of the Lord's blessings favoring the people, while Isaiah follows his passage in 2:6 with warnings of a punishment on the day of the coming of the Lord. Micah declares the Lord has decreed the people will live in peace, undisturbed under their own vines. Although other nations continue to follow their own gods, Israel will walk with faith in the Lord, the God of Israel, forever. On the day of the Lord, the Lord will gather the lame, the outcast, and the afflicted and give them new life. The lame and the weak, the surviving remnant, will become a strong nation with the Lord as the king on Mount Zion, forever.

Micah refers to Jerusalem as "daughter Zion," a female image occasionally used for Jerusalem, and proclaims dominion shall be restored to the city. The people cry out like a woman in labor, bemoaning their plight with no king and no one to lead them. Micah tells them to continue in their anguish, like a woman giving birth. He tells the people going into exile in Babylon that they will be rescued by the Lord.

Many nations are joining forces against Jerusalem, gloating over the downfall of Zion. These nations, however, are unaware of the plan of the Lord. Micah speaks the Word of the Lord, saying the Lord has gathered the nations like sheaves on the threshing floor and directed the Israelites to thresh them. The horn of Zion will be as sturdy as iron. The image of the horn refers to a powerful bull's horn and is often used as an image of strength. The horses' hooves will be like bronze to pulverize many people.

The Lord foresees the day when the people of Zion will offer their spoils of war and their wealth to the Lord of the whole earth, meaning the great God over all the gods. The Lord declares the present is a time for grieving, a time for suffering pain and the insult of being struck on the cheek. In striking the people of Zion, the enemy is striking the ruler of the people, namely the Lord.

In chapter 5, the Lord speaks of Bethlehem-Ephrathah, the place of King David's birth (see Ruth 1:2 and 1 Samuel 17:12), as the least of the clans of Judah and the place from which the ruler of Israel, whose origins are ancient, will come forth for the Lord. The message foreshadows the coming of the Messiah who will belong to the line of David. The entire passage has overtones relating to the coming Messiah.

The Lord will abandon the land of Israel until she who is to give birth has done so. She who is to give birth may be a reference to the mother of the Messiah. In the total context, the Lord is promising a day of rebirth for the nation. A remnant of the people of Judah shall return home, and the ideal Davidic king, with the strong support of the Lord, will take his place as a shepherd. The Lord's power, which reaches to the ends of the earth, will enable the people of Judah to live with security. The shepherd shall bring peace.

If Assyria invades the country, the shepherd will appoint seven shepherds, eight of royal status, who shall rise up against the Assyrians and destroy them when they tread upon the borders of Judah. The reference to seven and eight means a sufficient number will join in the uprising. The influence of the remnant of Jacob shall invigorate the nations like dew or showers on grass. Israel shall be like a lion among the nations or among submissive sheep. All her enemies will be torn apart and no one can rescue them. Judah shall be lifted above its foes, and all its enemies shall be cut down.

On that day, the Lord will destroy the horses, ruin their chariots, annihilate the cities, and tear down their fortresses. Soothsayers shall cease to exist. The Lord will destroy their carved images and sacred stones, and the people will no longer worship the idols shaped by their hands. The Lord will destroy their idols and act with anger against the nations refusing to listen.

Lectio Divina

Spend 8 to 10 minutes in silent contemplation of the following passage:

In his Gospel, Matthew describes the Magi as going to Jerusalem to ask about the birthplace of the newborn King of the Jews. The chief priests and scribes of the people answer their questions by quoting from the Book of Micah, saying, "And you, Bethlehem, land of Judah, are by no means least among the rulers of Judah; since from you shall come a ruler, who is to shepherd my people Israel" (Matthew 2:6). The people of Micah's era sought peace and the prophet offers them a spiritual peace by predicting a shepherd who will bring peace. The peace Jesus offers is an inner peace that remains, even in the midst of turmoil.

✠ *What can I learn from this passage?*

Day 4: True Worship of the Lord (Micah 6—7:6)

Micah bids the people to listen to the Word of the Lord. Using the imagery of a law court, the Lord summons the people to stand up and plead their case before the mountains, hills, and foundations of the earth that stand as witnesses. The Lord is the prosecutor and judge while Israel is the defendant. The Lord testifies against Israel, asking what made them become weary of their covenant with the Lord.

Pointing to three occasions in the past, the Lord demonstrates how the Israelites were helped. When Israel was in slavery in Egypt, the Lord sent Moses, Aaron, and Miriam to free them. Later, when the Moabite king wanted Balaam, a diviner, to curse the Israelites, the Lord forced Balaam to bless them. When the Israelites crossed the Jordan under the leadership of Joshua, the Lord dried up a path through the Jordan from Shittim to Gilgal to allow them to cross into the Promised Land.

Speaking in the name of the Israelites, Micah asks what he shall bring as he bows before the Lord in homage. He asks if he is to come with burnt offerings or year-old calves, with thousands of rams or countless streams of oil, or his firstborn, the fruit of his body, for the crime he has committed. Some of the Israelites, who worshiped false gods, offered their children as a sacrifice to the gods. The Lord replies they have already been told what is good and what the Lord requires. The Lord desires the Israelites to practice justice, to love goodness, and to walk humbly in the Lord's presence.

An insert in the text by a later editor declares it to be prudent to fear the name of the Lord. The Lord cries out to Jerusalem, asking what reaction the people expect from the Lord. Should the Lord accept hoarding or cheating when measuring out a short bushel, or crooked scales, or bags of false weights? The Lord accuses the wealthy of violence, speaking falsehood, and deceitful words.

The Lord is beginning to afflict the people of Jerusalem with destruction because of their sins. They will eat food that does not satisfy them, and what little they acquire will be taken by the sword. They shall sow, but not reap, and tread out olives, yet no oil, crush grapes, yet drink no wine. Before the final Assyrian invasion in 721 BC, the Assyrians occasionally harassed the northern kingdom of Israel, often seizing their crops. The Lord accuses the Israelites of following the ways of King Omri and his son Ahab, who supported idol worship in Israel. Because of the sin of the Israelites, the Lord will no longer support the nation, delivering the citizens to the contempt and reproach of other nations.

In chapter 7, Micah speaks as one deeply depressed because of the sinfulness he encounters. He compares himself to a person who attempts to gather summer fruit after the vines have been picked. He finds no cluster of fruit to eat, no early fig which he craves. The faithful and justice have disappeared from the land. The people plan to shed blood, each one ensnaring the other. The king places heavy demands on them, judges are bought for a price, and the powerful can say whatever they want with no one to confront them. The good, honest people will be like a briar or a thorn hedge in their midst, challenging their sinful actions. The sentinels (prophets) announce a day of punishment, a time for confusion. No one can be trusted, not a friend, not a loved one, not the son who belittles his father, not the daughter who rises up against her mother, and the daughter-in-law who rises up against her mother-in-law. Their enemies are members of their household.

Lectio Divina

Spend 8 to 10 minutes in silent contemplation of the following passage:

The trial portrayed in Micah 6—7 demonstrates how easily the people can forget all the Lord did for their nation. The Lord blessed them abundantly, but they turned away from the Lord and became engulfed in cheating, deception, and killing. The goods of the earth became more important than the blessings of knowing and serving the Lord.

All of us face the challenge of continually recalling all the Lord has done for us. It is so easy to become entangled in the material needs of our life that we forget the blessings the Lord gives us each day. In both difficult and joyful moments of life, we must pause and recall the blessings God has given to us.

✠ *What can I learn from this passage?*

Day 5: Confidence in the Future (Micah 7:7–20)

The Israelites respond to the Lord's indictment against them. They will wait for the Lord, their savior, who will hear them. Although they have fallen, they warn the enemy not to rejoice over them, because they will arise. Though they sit in darkness, the Lord is their light. Because of their sins against the Lord, they will endure the anger of the Lord. They will wait for the Lord to plead their cause and establish their rights again. When the Lord brings the Israelites to the light, they will then witness the Lord's righteousness.

When the enemy sees how well the Lord treats the Israelites, they will be overcome with shame. To mock the Israelites, they once asked where the God of Israel was. The Israelites shall witness the downfall of their enemies, trampled like mud in the streets. For the Israelites, the day of the Lord will be a day for building walls and enlarging boundaries. On that day, the remnant from Egypt to Assyria, from Tyre to the river (Euphrates), from sea to sea, and from mountain to mountain will come to Zion. Because of the evil deeds of the once-powerful nations, their land shall become a waste.

In 7:14, Micah prays to the Lord to shepherd the flock, the heritage of the Lord, with the shepherd's staff. The people will live in an orchard in the fertile lands of Bashan and Gilead as in ancient days. The prayer begs the Lord to perform miraculous signs as the Lord did when leading the people from the land of Egypt. The nations who oppressed the Israelites will witness the deeds of the Lord and, despite their power, will be put to shame. They will become speechless, unable to hear, crawling in the dust like a snake, and trembling in fear before the Lord.

In his prayer, Micah proclaims there is no God like the God of Jacob, who removes guilt, pardons the sins of the remnant, replaces anger with mercy, and tramples underfoot the sins of the people. The Lord casts the sins of Israel into the depths of the sea and shows faithfulness to the offspring of Jacob and Abraham, just as the Lord swore to their ancestors.

Lectio Divina

Spend 8 to 10 minutes in silent contemplation of the following passage:

The Israelites trust that a loving and compassionate God will forgive their sins if they sincerely repent of their past sinful actions. Christians live with the same assurance of forgiveness for those who honestly confess their sinfulness and attempt to live a life faithful to the Lord in the future. The compassionate and forgiving nature of God is often taken for granted, but it is one of the great blessings the Lord grants us.

✠ *What can I learn from this passage?*

Review Questions

1. What do we learn about the relationship between Edom and Judah in the Book of Obadiah?
2. Why does Micah lament over the Israelites?
3. What does Micah say about the leaders of the Israelites?
4. What does Micah say about the compassion and forgiveness of God?

The Books of Nahum, Habakkuk, and Zephaniah

For though the fig tree does not blossom, and no fruit appears on the vine, Though the yield of the olive fails and the terraces produce no nourishment, Though the flocks disappear from the fold and there is no herd in the stalls, Yet I will rejoice in the LORD and exult in my saving God (Habakkuk 3:17–18).

Opening Prayer (SEE PAGE 15)

Context

Part 1: Nahum The Book of Nahum, which appears to have been written shortly before the fall of Assyria in 612 BC, rejoices over the impending doom of savage Assyria. In 722-721 BC, Assyria invaded the northern kingdom of Israel, slaughtering many of the inhabitants, sending some of the survivors into exile, and importing other conquered people into the territory. They invaded Jerusalem shortly before 700 BC and compelled many of the cities of Judah to become vassals of Assyria. Nineveh, which was destroyed in 612 BC, was the capital of Assyria, and its fall under the stronger armies of the Medes and Babylonians marked the end of the Assyrian empire. The Book of Nahum addresses the fall of Nineveh and the restoration of Judah.

Part 2: Habakkuk, Zephaniah The Book of Habakkuk devotes its entire material to issues concerning the Lord's management of worldly events. It consists of a dialogue between Habakkuk and God. Habakkuk speaks about Babylon's defeat of the Egyptian army in 605 BC and the second Babylonian invasion of Judah in 587 BC. The conditions in Judah lead to Habakkuk's questions about divine justice.

The Book of Zephaniah speaks of the day of the Lord, a day of dire judgment for Judah and Jerusalem. Zephaniah lived during the early years of King Josiah of Judah, who reigned from 640 to 609 BC. He apparently prophesied before King Josiah began a major reform in 621 BC. Zephaniah views the worship of idols and the obnoxious injustice of the leaders of Judah as the reason for the Lord's punishment of Judah and Jerusalem.

PART 1: GROUP STUDY (NAHUM)

Read aloud the Book of Nahum.

1—2:1 Judgment Against Nineveh

The oracle of the Lord concerning Nineveh comes from the prophet Nahum, who is identified in the opening verse as the source of the message. Nothing else is known about him. In his oracle of the Lord, he describes the cosmic effects of the coming of the Lord.

Nahum speaks of the Lord as a jealous and avenging God who is slow to anger but full of power, punishing the guilty. As Lord of heaven and earth, the Lord God comes among the people in a storm wind and tempest, moving with the clouds like dust underfoot and roaring at the sea and rivers, which dry up, and the lush lands of Bashan, Carmel, and Lebanon, which wither. Before the Lord, the mountains quake, the hills dissolve, the earth, the world, and all who dwell in it are ravaged. The prophet asks who could remain unbending, enduring the blazing anger of the Lord. Like fire, the fury of the Lord spreads across the land, breaking boulders in its wake. On the day of distress, when floods rage, the Lord will protect those who are faithful. The Lord will destroy every opponent, tracking them into the darkness.

Nahum asks the people of Nineveh what they are plotting against the Lord, who is about to destroy them. No opponent has a second chance. The Lord's opponents are like branches tangled in a thorny thicket, as drunk as drunkards, and as utterly consumed as dry stubble. Nineveh is plotting evil against the Lord, and the Lord—knowing their strength and their numbers—will destroy them so they will disappear from the earth.

The Lord then speaks to Judah. The Lord once humbled the people of Judah, but the Lord will humble them no longer. The Lord will break the Assyrian yoke off their backs and tear away their bonds. A yoke symbolizes the dominion of Assyria over Judah. The Lord decrees the total annihilation of the Assyrians, with no descendants ever coming from them again. The Lord will eradicate the carved and molten images of their gods and turn their graves into a dung heap.

The one bearing the good news of peace will come across the mountains. Judah can again celebrate her feasts with joy and live faithfully dedicated to the covenant. The destroyers, the Assyrians, will never again invade the land. They are totally annihilated.

2:2—3 Nineveh's Fate

Nahum declares the one who scatters shall come up against the people of Nineveh. The reference of the one who scatters could be to the Medes or Babylonians. Nahum instructs the people of Nineveh to prepare for battle, guarding the barricades, watching the road, bracing themselves, marshaling their strength. The next line in the prophesy appears to be an addition by a later editor, since it turns attention to Judah, saying the Lord will restore the vine of Judah and the honor of Israel because ravagers have plundered them and destroyed their branches.

The text returns to the original call to battle. The shields of the warriors are crimsoned, the soldiers are clad in scarlet, the chariots are shining like fire, and the cavalry stirring in anticipation. When the battle begins, the chariots madly charge through the streets and squares like torches and bolts of lightning. The special forces of the enemy break rank for the charge, rushing at the wall, their protective screen moving with them. Nineveh has a tributary of the Tigris River running through the center of the town. The river gates are opened, and the palace is washed away. Opening the gates may somehow have led to the flooding of the town.

"The mistress," a symbol for either the city of Nineveh or her queen, is led into captivity with her maidservants, all moaning like doves and beating their breasts as an expression of fear and humiliation. Nineveh is covered with floodwaters, prompting the people of Nineveh to plead for an end to the siege, but no one listens. The invading army plunders the silver, gold, and every form of treasure.

Nineveh becomes a scene of emptiness, desolation, waste, fainting hearts, trembling knees, stomachs churning from fright, and every face turning pale from fear. Nahum speaks of a lioness and lion who are killed, an apparent reference to the queen and king who were once able to move about freely, like a lion going in and out of its cave. Since the lion was also a symbol for Assyria, this passage could be a reference to the total destruction of Assyria rather than its leaders. The lion once had no qualms about savagely tearing apart the enemy. Using the power of the invading army, the Lord battles against the Assyrians, destroying their chariots and killing their young. In this final defeat of the Assyrians, their preying on neighboring nations comes to an end.

In chapter 3, Nahum continues to speak of Assyria as though it still exists, thus the oracles do not follow a chronological order. He talks of Assyria as a bloody city, full of deceit and ceaseless plunder and pictures the scene with sounds and sight, a crack of the whip, rumbling wheels, horses galloping, chariots clattering, cavalry charging, swords flashing, spears gleaming, and an endless mass of bodies over which the warriors stumble. He declares Assyria was like a prostitute, a charming woman who enslaved nations with her prostitution and her enemies with her witchcraft. Using the image of punishment of a prostitute who would have her dress lifted up above her face, exposing her in shame, the Lord will also expose Assyria in shame to the nations, making the nation a spectacle to other nations. Her shame will cause others to run from her, crying out that Nineveh is destroyed. No one will pity her.

Nahum asks the Assyrians if they thought they were greater than a city in Egypt named No, whose god was known as Amon. The name No-amon was the capital of Upper Egypt and known as Thebes to the Greeks. It was set among the canals of the Nile, protected by the waters surrounding it like walls. Egypt, Ethiopia, the nation of Put in North Africa, and the Libyans were great cities which were captured. The people of No-amon went into exile as captives. Their defense was so weak they could not protect their infants, who were slaughtered in the city. The conquering army cast lots to take their nobles as slaves. All the great ones of No-amon were put in chains.

Nahum predicts the Assyrians will drink of this destruction and seek refuge from the enemy. Their fortresses are like fig trees, bearing early figs. The early figs are a reference to those who escaped from Nineveh only to be captured later. When the fig trees are shaken, the figs (refugees) fall into the mouth of those seeking to consume them. The troops of the Assyrians become like a weak army of women. The gates, which ordinarily protected them, will be thrust open and burned.

Nahum speaks sarcastically, telling the people of Nineveh to draw water for the siege, strengthen their fortresses, and make bricks, all futile and pointless tasks in the face of their destruction. The fire will consume them, and they will die by the sword which will destroy them like grasshoppers. He mockingly adds they should multiply like grasshoppers or locusts, knowing this will still not be enough. Their many merchants, as numerous as the stars of the heavens, act like grasshoppers that shed their skin and fly away.

The sentinels and scribes of Assyria become like locust swarms which inhabit the fences on a cold day and vanish when the sun rises, with no one knowing where they went. They abandon the city. The fate of Nineveh is hopeless, with their shepherds (leaders) slumbering and their nobles resting, abandoning their role of leadership and leaving the people scattered upon the mountains with no one to gather them together. Their wound (defeat) is fatal, with no way to heal it. All those who hear the news of the fall of Assyria clap their hands in joy, for all have suffered under Assyria's endless evil.

Review Questions

1. Does the Lord's destruction of Assyria as found in the Book of Nahum point to a vengeful God?
2. Why was Assyria called "blood city?"
3. How does the image of grasshoppers and locusts fit Nahum's message?

Closing Prayer (SEE PAGE 15)

Pray the closing prayer now or after *lectio divina*.

Lectio Divina (SEE PAGE 8)

Relax your body and maintain a posture of prayer (back straight, eyes shut, feet flat on the floor). This exercise can take as long as you want, but in the context of this Bible study, 10 to 20 minutes should be sufficient.

The meditations that follow are provided only to help group participants use this prayer form, but note that lectio is intended to bring one to a place of prayerful contemplation where the Word of God speaks to the hearer from his or her heart. (See page 8 for further instruction.)

Judgment Against Nineveh (1—2:1)

A well-known proverb states, "If God is for us, who can be against us?" Nahum speaks of the power of the Lord over all creation and the foolishness of attempting to defeat the people the Lord protects. In ancient times, the people of Israel believed God would protect them, if not in their own lifetime, then in a later generation. Protection of the name of the nation was important to them. They realized they had to be patient when they prayed.

Praying with patience and trust is difficult for people today who seek immediate results. We can learn from St. Monica the need for trust and patience in prayer. She prayed forty years for her son, Augustine, to accept Christ. When Augustine did accept the Lord, he became a great saint. Saint Monica really believed, "If God is for us, who can be against us?" When she prayed, God was for her and her son. When the Israelites prayed, it was with a hope that the Lord would protect their nation from complete annihilation.

✠ *What can I learn from this passage?*

Nineveh's Fate (2:2—3)

Using peaceful means in striving for a specific goal is often more successful than the sword. Leaders who used peaceful means rather than the sword had a major influence on the history of their nation. Martin Luther King Jr. helped to bring racial equality in America; Mahatma Gandhi helped bring independence to his nation in India, and Nelson Mandela helped bring equality for all people in South Africa. They did not live by the sword. Their weapons of peaceful demonstrations and faith changed history.

✠ *What can I learn from this passage?*

PART 2: INDIVIDUAL STUDY (HABAKKUK, ZEPHANIAH)

Day 1: God's Rule in the World (Habakkuk 1—2:1)

The opening sentence identifies Habakkuk as the source of the material found in this book. An oracle of the Lord comes to him in a vision.

Habakkuk complains the Lord does not listen when he cries out for help or warns about violence. He asks why the Lord allows him to endure all this wickedness while the Lord just gazes on it, doing nothing. He claims the law is ineffective and justice does not exist. Because "the wicked surround the just," justice cannot function. Habakkuk finds the Lord's lack of concern frustrating.

The Lord responds to Habakkuk's complaint, instructing him to look in amazement at the great work taking place throughout the nations, something he would not believe if he were just told about it. The Lord speaks of raising up the Chaldeans (Babylonians), a harsh and impulsive people who march over the land, plundering nations. The Lord chose the Chaldeans to punish the people of Judah. The Lord informs Habakkuk the Chaldeans have established their own reputation as a terrifying and dreadful nation. The reference points to the Chaldean conquest of the Egyptian army in 605 BC.

The Lord speaks to Habakkuk about the overwhelming power of the Chaldeans. They come from far away on horses swifter than leopards and desert wolves and fly like an eagle rushing to consume prey. Their violent attacks are like a storm wind that gathers up captives like sand. They mock kings, ridicule princes, scoff at fortifications, build earthen ramps, and conquer fortresses. They defeat a number of kings and nobles in their surge across the nations, giving the impression no fortification could deter them.

The Lord informs Habakkuk the Chaldeans tear through the land like the wind and vanish. They surge into the land, ravage it and the people, and leave the local rulers to clean up the damage. They would often make the conquered lands vassals of Babylon, forcing them to pay tribute to their nation. Like all the people of the era, the Chaldeans viewed their power as coming from the gods they worshiped.

Habakkuk speaks again to the Lord, whom he addresses as the Lord from of old, the holy God, immortal. Referring to the Lord as "Rock," he notes the Lord has appointed the Chaldeans to punish Judah. When David was dying, he referred to the Lord as "the Rock of Israel" who was the "one who rules over humankind with justice" (see 2 Samuel 23:3). Although Habakkuk does not refer to 2 Samuel when applying the term "Rock" to the Lord, he is stressing the Lord, the immovable "Rock," is the one who rules with justice.

Despite Habakkuk's belief the Lord rules with justice, he says the Lord is too pure and cannot endure the sight of evil. His words reflect the thoughts of Psalm 5:5 which declares the Lord does not delight in evil. Admitting that Judah is not innocent and has shown herself to be faithless, Habakkuk asks why the Lord is allowing those who are more wicked to devour her. Without waiting for an answer to his question, Habakkuk compares human beings to fish in the sea or crawling things that have no leader. The Chaldeans, like a fisherman who casts his net and hook into the sea, catches the Judeans and hauls them away like fish in their fishing net.

The net apparently refers to the strength of the Chaldeans, which they arrogantly worship as their god. The captured Judeans, like fish caught and eaten, satisfy the arrogance of the Chaldeans. Habakkuk asks the Lord if they will continue to destroy nations without mercy.

Habakkuk ends this part of his complaint by picturing himself as a sentry standing on the fortification, prepared to hear what the Lord will say concerning his complaint.

Lectio Divina

Spend 8 to 10 minutes in silent contemplation of the following passage:

> A woman once said to her friend, "I really don't understand how a loving God could allow so much suffering in the world." Her concern sounds very much like that of Habakkuk, who wondered why the Lord seemed to make things so difficult for the people of Judah. According to the Scriptures, the Lord takes no pleasure in the suffering of people, but in many cases (not all) suffering draws out the best in people. Trusting God in the midst of suffering is one of the greatest tests of our faith and dedication.

✠ *What can I learn from this passage?*

Day 2: God's Response (Habakkuk 2:2–20)

The Lord instructed Habakkuk to write down the vision clearly on a tablet so a runner who reads it may bring it to others. In ancient times, runners were commonly used to deliver a message from one place to another. Writing the vision on a tablet allowed it to be verified when the prophecy in the vision was fulfilled. The Lord pledges the day of fulfillment would come, and if it is delayed, the people are to wait for it. The proud have no integrity, but just ones will live because they are patient and faithful.

The Lord declares wealth is treacherous and the proud are destined to fail. They open their mouths like Sheol (the place of the dead) and find their appetite for wealth as insatiable as death. The words refer to the Chaldeans, who gather as many nations and peoples as they can to themselves. All these nations will scoff at their conquerors in the end, asking how long they expect to store up all that does not belong to them.

The Lord declares a time will come when these debtors (the conquered nations) will awake and rise up, making the Chaldeans tremble with fear. In return for all the plundering and slaughtering the Chaldeans did, these nations will plunder and slaughter them. The Lord accuses the Chaldeans of pursuing evil gain for themselves, seeking to live in grandeur, far from misfortune. In their conquests, they created shame for themselves, forfeiting their own life for ravaging the life of others.

The Lord next speaks of a building as though it were human, with the stone in the wall crying out and the beam in the frame declaring the city was built with the shedding of blood. That which the people toil to build is consumed by the flames. Since the Chaldeans will destroy their town, the people of the nations wear themselves out for nothing. In the end, the earth shall be filled with the knowledge of the Lord's glory, as sure as waters cover the sea.

The Lord addresses the nation of the Chaldeans as those who make the neighboring nations drunk on the wrath of their army and expose the nakedness of their captives to others. Now they will experience shame, not glory. The Lord turns their own evil on them, extolling them to drink the cup of the wrath of the Lord and stagger like a drunken people. The violence done to the lush land of Lebanon and the annihilation of the animals in its forests will lead to their terrifying destruction. When they built their magnificent palaces, the Chaldeans hacked down the cedar forests of Lebanon and hunted for wild animals.

The Lord stresses the uselessness of idol worship. The Chaldeans use carved images and molten images that are mute idols made by human hands. They cry out to the wood to awake and the stone to arise, but they remain silent, unable to give any oracles. Overlaid with gold and silver, they lack breath. The Lord, however, is in the holy Temple of God, and all the earth falls silent before the Lord.

Lectio Divina

Spend 8 to 10 minutes in silent contemplation of the following passage:

In the total context of creation, life is short. The Chaldeans grasped as much wealth as they could, but like many people with wealth, what they had did not satisfy them and they wanted more. Unfortunately for them, the Lord cried, "Enough," and their wealth and conquests became their conquerors.

When people spend their lives hurting others in their attempt to gain more possessions, they soon learn power or wealth does not satisfy them. In the end, they no longer control their wealth, but their wealth controls them and causes them to seek more wealth, no matter how much it hurts them or others. Wealth used wisely and generously to help others can bring satisfaction and contentment, but a person who seeks wealth for the sake of wealth is already destined to an unfulfilled life.

✠ *What can I learn from this passage?*

___

Day 3: Jerusalem Reproached (Habakkuk 3)

This is a psalm of Habakkuk, the prophet, according to Shigyonot. The meaning of Shigyonot is not known, although many commentators suspect it is some type of liturgical or musical direction for praying the psalm that follows. "Selah" appears three times in this passage, as though it were a refrain, supporting the idea the psalm may have been used in worship.

Habakkuk expresses his awe over the deeds he heard the Lord achieved for the people in the past and pleads with the Lord to again perform these good works for the sake of bringing renewed praise to the Lord. Conscious of the anger the Lord has against Judah for her sins, he begs the Lord to show compassion as in the past.

Habakkuk then proclaims the Lord, the Holy One, comes to the people from Teman and Mount Paran, two cities in Edom. The route taken by the Lord points to the Lord's visitation coming from the direction of Mount Sinai. In this visitation, the glory of the Lord covers the heavens; the praise of the Lord fills the earth, and the splendor of the Lord spreads like light. The image may be drawn from the figure of a Phoenician storm god, who is depicted as holding a lightning bolt in his hand.

Habakkuk describes pestilence and plague as part of the Lord's entourage, foreshadowing the catastrophe about to strike the enemy. Like a warrior, the Lord stands and shakes the earth, and under the gaze of the Lord, nations tremble. Ancient mountains shatter, ancient hills sink low, and ancient orbits collapse. The collapsing orbits refer to the daily paths taken by the sun, moon, and stars. Habakkuk speaks of fear gripping the people in an unknown place named Cushan, located in the land of Midian. Habakkuk continues to view the route taken by the Lord as coming from Mount Sinai.

Ancient Canaan myths pictured battles taking place between the divinity and the rivers. The cosmic war occurs when the rivers and sea disrupt the order of creation, causing chaos by spilling over their boundaries. Like a warrior mounted on steeds and charging in a chariot, the Lord attacks the rivers and sea, fighting with bow and arrows. The imagery of arrows refers to lightning. The Lord splits the earth with rivers, and at the sight of the Lord, the mountains shake. A downpour follows and the rushing waters create a deafeningly roar. Because of the lightning, portrayed as the dazzling light of flying arrows and the Lord's flashing spear, the sun does not appear to rise and the moon leaves its place.

In anger, the Lord marches on the earth and tramples the nations. The Lord, the Creator of the world, comes forward to save the anointed one (Judah) who is the head of the Lord's people and to crush the back of the wicked one (the Chaldeans). The Lord pierces the head of the enemy with shafts, scattering their leaders with the violence of a storm wind. The Lord tramples the sea with horses, churning up the depths, symbolically overcoming the power of the chaos of the deep. In ancient times, the people of Judah believed evil spirits dwelt in the watery depths.

When Habakkuk hears of the Lord's wrath, his body quakes, his lips quiver, and his legs tremble. His fear and anxiety come from his expectation of the day of distress soon to afflict the enemy who attacked them.

With extravagant images, Habakkuk proclaims his trust in the Lord.

"For though the fig tree does not blossom, and no fruit appears on the vine, Though the yield of the olive fails and the terraces produce no nourishment, Though the flocks disappear from the fold and there is no herd in the stalls," he will still profess his joy in the Lord and exult in his saving God (3:17). The Lord God makes the feet of the prophet as swift as those of a deer that enable him to walk on the heights. The passage ends with a short remark giving directions to the leader of the assembly concerning the use of stringed instruments when praying Habakkuk's psalm.

Lectio Divina

Spend 8 to 10 minutes in silent contemplation of the following passage:

Habakkuk's prayer recognizes the Lord as the one and only powerful God of the universe. No matter how difficult life may become, he professes he will never lose faith in the Lord. His words sound very much like the words of Paul the Apostle, who spoke of his dedication to the Lord, no matter what happens to him. He writes: "For I am convinced that neither death, nor life, nor angels, nor principalities, nor present things, nor future things, nor powers, nor height, nor depth, nor any other creature will be able to separate us from the love of God in Christ Jesus our Lord" (Romans 8:38–39). The dedication of Habakkuk and Paul the Apostle challenges everyone who reads the Bible to remain faithful to the Lord, no matter what happens.

✠ *What can I learn from this passage?*

Day 4: Judgment on Judah (Zephaniah 1—3:5)

The book traces Zephaniah's lineage back four generations to ancestor Hezekiah, who most likely was King Hezekiah who ruled in Judah from 715 to 687 BC. Tracing a lineage back four generations would be unlikely unless the book wished to show that Zephaniah comes from a royal line.

The Lord threatens the people of Judah with complete annihilation, pledging to sweep away everything in Judah, including human beings, birds, and fish. The wicked will stumble and all people will disappear from the land. In Judah and Jerusalem, the Lord will destroy the last vestiges of Baal, including the priests serving the idols, the idolaters on their roofs who worship the sun, moon, stars, and planets, those who worship the Lord of Israel but swear by Milcom, the god of the Ammonites, and those who turned away from the Lord with no intention of returning.

Zephaniah instructs the people to remain silent in the presence of the Lord and warns the day of the Lord is near. He presents an image of the Lord preparing a sacrifice for consecrated guests, a reference to nations other than Israel who are like offerings consecrated for sacrifice. On the day of sacrifice, the Lord will punish the officials, the king's sons, and all who dress like their foreign invaders, probably a reference to those who wear vestments for pagan rituals.

Zephaniah proclaims the Lord will punish those who "leap over the threshold" (1:9), a religious practice of the Philistine priests, and those who fill their master's house with violence and deceit. The violence refers to those who practice injustice, and deceit refers to those who worship false gods. Wailing will be heard from various locations, including the Fish gate, the Second Quarter, the hills, and the inhabitants of Maktesh, yet another part of Jerusalem, over the annihilation of the merchants who deal in silver and gold.

Using the image of a man searching in dark corners with lamps, the Lord will search out all the evildoers in Jerusalem and punish those who settle like dregs in wine, a reference to the complacency of those who do not believe the Lord will do anything, neither good nor harm. The Lord declares their wealth and the houses they build will be plundered and devastated. They will build houses and not live in them, plant vineyards and not drink their wine.

The day of the Lord is coming swiftly and will resound with a piercing sound. Zephaniah presents one of the most devastating images of the judgment of the Lord. The day of the Lord's wrath will be a day of distress and anguish, of ruin and desolation, of darkness and gloom, and of thick black clouds, blasts of the trumpet, and battle cries against great fortifications. The Lord will surround the people so they will walk like the blind because of their sins against the Lord. The Lord will pour out their blood like dust. Silver and gold will be unable to save them. Payments of silver and gold were often used to bribe an enemy to avoid destruction or in payment for an alliance with another nation against an enemy. On the day of the Lord's wrath, the earth will be consumed in the fire of his passion, and all people on earth will meet with a sudden end.

In chapter 2, Zephaniah calls the people to gather together before they become extinct, like chaff that disappears or before the Lord's blazing anger destroys them. He addresses the people of Judah as a nation without shame. Turning his attention to the good people of the land who humbly observe the law, he urges them to seek the Lord, justice, and humility. He offers them the hope of being sheltered on the day of the Lord's fury.

Zephaniah names Philistine cities that will also be destroyed. Canaan, a land of the Philistines, will be destroyed, leaving the land as fields for shepherds and their flocks. The seacoast shall be a haven for the remnant of Judah. They shall pasture their sheep by the sea and rest in the house of Ashkelon, another conquered city. The Lord has heard the taunts of the people of Moab and the Ammonites against the people of God, and, in retaliation, the Lord shall make Moab like Sodom and the Ammonites like Gomorrah. They will become a field of weeds, a wasteland and salt pit. The remnant of the Lord's people will plunder them and dispossess them. Because they taunted and boasted against the Lord's people, this will be a recompense for their arrogance. They will become terrified as all the gods on earth waste away. The distant nations, remaining in their land, will bow down to the Lord of Israel.

The Lord warns the Cushites (Ethiopians) they will be slain by the sword. The Lord will reach to the north and make Assyria, with its capital at Nineveh, a wasteland. Flocks and wildlife will inhabit it. Zephaniah pictures owls roosting in the land as conversing with the raven. They ask if this land were the exultant city, once so secure, that boasted of its glory above all other nations. They ask how it became such a wasteland, such a lair for wild animals, that those who pass by hiss and shake their fists, gestures meant to ward off evil spirits dwelling in the desert wasteland.

Chapter 3 begins with Zephaniah reproaching Jerusalem, addressing it as a rebellious, polluted, and tyrannical city, listening to no one and accepting no correction. The city did not draw near or trust the Lord. Its rulers have devoured them like roaring lions and its judges consumed them like desert wolves until no bones for gnawing are left by morning. Its prophets are treacherous. Its priests profane what is holy and treat the law with violence. The Lord, in the midst of the land, renders judgment morning after morning without fail, but the wicked know no shame.

Day 5: Judgment on the Nations (Zephaniah 3:6–20)

In verse 6, the Lord begins to speak in the first person. The Lord devastated the other nations for Jerusalem, destroying their defenses. Their land becomes a wasteland, with their streets deserted and their cities devastated. The Lord cries out to Jerusalem, expecting they will surely respond in awe and accept corrections in light of all the good they received from the Lord. Surprisingly, they more willingly became corrupt.

The Lord continues, telling the people of Judah to wait for the day the Lord becomes their accuser. The Lord plans to gather nations and kingdoms and pour out on them the fire of the Lord's wrath and burning anger, which will consume all the earth.

A sudden reversal will take place as the Lord purifies other nations so they will call on the name of the Lord and serve the Lord as one people. From beyond Ethiopia and from faraway lands in the North, they shall bring offerings to the Lord. On that day, the people of Jerusalem will no longer need to be ashamed of all their rebellious deeds against the Lord. The Lord will remove from their midst the arrogant who exalt themselves on the Lord's holy mountain.

The Lord pledges to leave in the land a humble and lowly people, a remnant of Israel who shall take refuge in the name of the Lord. They shall do no wrong, speak no lies, and be cleansed of deceit. They shall pasture and lie down in security, with no one to disturb them.

Zephaniah calls upon daughter Zion to shout for joy, Israel to sing joyfully, and Jerusalem to rejoice with all her heart. The Lord has removed the judgment against them and turned away their enemies. The King of Israel, the Lord, is in their midst, protecting them against any future misfortune. On that day, Jerusalem (Zion) shall receive word not to fear or be discouraged. The Lord their God, a mighty savior, is in their midst, rejoicing over them, renewing the love relationship with the nation, and celebrating their feasts with them.

The Lord promises to remove disaster from them so no one can speak about their shameful destruction. At that time, the Lord will deal harshly with all their oppressors. The Lord promises to save the lame, assemble the outcasts, and bring praise and renown to the nation of Judah in every land where they were once shamed. The Lord will gather them from among the nations and bring them to their homeland. When the nations witness the restoration they obtain from the Lord who is in their midst, they will receive glory and praise.

Lectio Divina

Spend 8 to 10 minutes in silent contemplation of the following passage:

> The parents of a nineteen-year-old boy worried about the reckless-ness of their son. For the second time, he was arrested for stealing. The first time he went to jail, the parents paid bail for his release. On this occasion, they decided not to pay bail, hoping a few days in jail would teach him a lesson. They knew jail would be difficult for him, but they decided to take the route of tough love.

> In the Book of Zephaniah, the Lord grew tired of bailing out the people of Judah, so the Lord allowed powerful nations to invade the country, kill many of the people, send others into exile, and devastate the land with the hope the people would learn their lesson and remain faithful to the covenant. After all the devasta-tion, the Lord redeemed the people, expressing the hope, "Surely now you will fear me, you will accept correction" (3:7). For many people, their most intense prayer conversion to God comes when they are experiencing some affliction, fear, rejection, or emotional pain in their life.

✠ *What can I learn from this passage?*

Review Questions

1. How does the Lord respond to Habakkuk's complaints?

2. How does Habakkuk's prayer praise the Lord and proclaim his trust in the Lord?

3. What do you consider to be the worst punishment of the Lord against Judah in the Book of Zephaniah?

4. What do you consider to be the worst punishment of the Lord against the nations in the Book of Zephaniah?

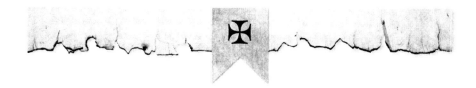

The Books of
Haggai and Zechariah (I)

HAGGAI AND ZECHARIAH 1—8

*For there will be a sowing of peace: the vine will yield its fruit,
the land will yield its crops, and the heavens will yield their dew
(Zechariah 8:12).*

Opening Prayer (SEE PAGE 15)

Context

Part 1: Haggai The Book of Haggai speaks of the period a little
more than a decade after the Jews returned from exile in Babylon,
when Darius I was king of Persia (522–486 BC). After their return
from exile in 538 BC, the people of Judah had begun to rebuild the
Temple in Jerusalem, but they were forced to end the reconstruction
until the reign of King Darius, who allowed them to continue. The
Lord tells the people to reflect on the struggles they have endured
and to know the reason for this scarcity of produce: They will once
again receive blessings when they rebuild the house of the Lord.

Part 2: Zechariah 1—8 The Book of Zechariah consists of at least
two separate segments, leading commentators to identify an early
prophet as First Zechariah (chapters 1—8) and a later prophet or
prophets as Second Zechariah (chapters 9—14). This chapter will
study First Zechariah, who was a contemporary of Haggai. He

centers his prophecies on Jerusalem, the leaders of the inhabitants, and the restoration of the Temple in Jerusalem beginning in 520 BC. An editor gathered together the prophecies and reforms of First Zechariah.

In chapters 1 through 8, Zechariah receives visions of an angel of the Lord who brings a message of the Lord to Zechariah with each vision. In the first vision, four riders patrol the earth to assess the situation. In the second vision, four horns representing the four powers are confronted by the Israelites and the Lord's punishment of them. In the third vision, a man with a measuring cord is like a surveyor who measures the length and width of Jerusalem. Joshua becomes the specially chosen high priest, and the Lord promises to restore the Davidic line. In the fourth vision, the Lord promises Zerubbabel, who began the restoration of the Temple, he would finish it. In the fifth vision, the Lord sends a large scroll, cursing every thief and those who swear falsely. In the sixth vision, the angels of the Lord gather a basket of wickedness for the temple in Babylon. In the seventh vision, the Lord sends four charioteers who will patrol the earth and bring the riches and the exiles back to Jerusalem. In the final vision, the Word of the Lord speaks of the joy of the return of the people from exile.

PART 1: GROUP STUDY (HAGGAI)

Read aloud the Book of Haggai.

1 Response of the Leaders and People

On the first day of the sixth month in the second year of Darius the king of Persia (August 29, 520 BC), the Word of the Lord came through the prophet Haggai to the governor of Judah, Zerubbabel, and to the high priest, Joshua. Darius I was the emperor of Persia from 522 to 486 BC. Since the land of Judah now belonged to the Persian Empire, the Jews followed the Persian custom of referring to a governor as the local ruler of a province. Zerubbabel was the grandson of King Jehoiachin, whom the king of Babylon sent into exile in Babylon (see 2 Kings 24:15), which made him a descendant of David.

Shortly after the return of the Jews from exile, a major debate among the returning remnant concerned the time for rebuilding the Temple. Haggai states the Lord of hosts said the people have decided it was not time to rebuild the house of the Lord. The foundations for the rebuilding of the Temple had begun to be laid in 536 BC, but King Artaxerxes of Persia, falsely warned by some opponents of the Jews that the Temple and the city would be used as a fortification in a rebellion against the Persians, ordered the rebuilding of the Temple and the city to cease. A later king, Darius, allowed the work to begin during Haggai's lifetime (see Ezra 4—6). The Lord questions whether the governor and the high priest should dwell in their paneled houses while the Temple lay in ruins.

Haggai passed on the Word of the Lord to Zerubbabel and Joshua, telling them to reflect on their recent experiences. They have sown much but harvested little, eaten without being satisfied, drunk without being intoxicated, clothed themselves without being warm, and hired workers "for a bag full of holes" (1:6), which means workers who brought in no gain. Instead of restoring the Temple on their return from exile, the people who could now rebuild the Temple were working hard on building a better life for themselves while neglecting the Temple. Despite their hard work, they gained very little from it.

Haggai again speaks the Word of the Lord, telling the people to reflect on their own experience. The Lord instructs the people to go into the hill country, gather timber, and build the house of the Lord so the Lord may be pleased and glorified. In the eyes of the nations, a temple of a god reflected the power and glory of the god. To restore glory to the Lord among the nations, the people have to construct a temple to the Lord.

The Lord accuses the people of expecting much, but what they received and what they brought home the Lord blew away, which means it all amounted to nothing. Because the people rushed to take care of their own house while the Temple lay in ruin, the Lord withheld the dew and the earth its harvest. The Lord cast a devastating heat on the land, on the mountains, the grain, the new wine, the olive oil, and all the growth of the land. Human beings, beasts, and all they produce also shared in the devastation.

Zerubbabel (the governor), Joshua (the high priest), and all the remnants of the people obeyed the Lord's message as given to them by Haggai, whom the people accepted as a prophet of the Lord. His words cause the people to fear the Lord. Haggai, again referred to as one sent by God, proclaims the message of the Lord, telling the people the Lord is with them.

The Lord then stirred up the spirit of Zerubbabel, Joshua, and the remnant of the people, so they began work on the house of the Lord on the twenty-fourth day of the sixth month in the second year of Darius, the king of Persia (September 21, 520 BC).

2 Assurance of God's Presence

On the twenty-first day of the seventh month (October 17, 520 BC), the Word of the Lord came through Haggai, directing him to speak to Zerubbabel, Joshua, and the remnant of the people, asking who among them had seen the house of the Lord in its former glory. The remnant consisted of people led into exile and those who remained in a devastated Jerusalem after the Babylonian invasion. A large number of the people of Judah lived in exile for fifty years, and the journey from Babylon to Judah was a long and arduous one. It would seem those who remembered the glory of the old Temple would be very elderly and therefore not likely to be the ones who traveled the long, hard journey from Babylon. They would be the ones who remained in Jerusalem after the Babylonian invasion.

The Lord asks the people if the construction of the Temple means nothing to them. In reality, the Lord is saying this is a day of glory for the Lord. Those sorrowing recalled the glory of the old Temple and grieved over its loss, while others not familiar with the old Temple cheered the laying of the foundation for the new. In the Book of Ezra we read: "Many of the priests, Levites, and heads of ancestral houses who were old enough to have seen the former house, cried out in sorrow as they watched the foundation for the present house being laid. Many others, however, lifted up their voices in shouts of joy" (Ezra 3:12).

The Lord bids Zerubbabel, Joshua, and all the people of the land to be strong and work on the Temple. The people of the land include not only the remnant but also those whom the Babylonians brought into Judah to intermarry with the conquered Jews. At this point in the history of Judah, they would have learned to worship the God of the Israelites. When the Israelites were led out of Egypt, the Lord told them not to fear, for the Lord God of hosts would remain with them.

Haggai, speaking the Word of the Lord, tells the people the Lord will shake heaven and earth, the sea and the dry land, and all the nations so the treasures of all nations will come to Judah and fill the house of the Lord with glory. Silver and gold will belong to the Lord. Isaiah the prophet predicted this when he said, "In days to come, the mountain of the Lord's house shall be established as the highest mountain and raised above the hills. All nations shall stream toward it" (Isaiah 2:2). Later, in the Book of Isaiah, we read: "Caravans of camels shall cover you, dromedaries of Midian and Ephah. All from Sheba shall come bearing gold and frankincense, and heralding the praises of the Lord" (Isaiah 60:6).

The Lord declares the glory of the new Temple will be greater than the former Temple, and with it, the Lord will bring peace to Judah.

On the twenty-fourth day of the ninth month in the second year of Darius (December 18, 520 BC), the Word of the Lord came to Haggai the prophet, directing him to bring two questions to the priests concerning sanctity and defilement. In the Book of Leviticus, the Lord tells the priestly family of Aaron, "You must be able to distinguish between what is sacred and what is profane, and between what is clean and what is unclean" (Leviticus 10:10). Since it is the duty of the priest to determine what is clean or unclean, the Lord, faithful to the law, sends Haggai to the priests for an answer.

Through the prophet Haggai, the Lord poses the first question. If a person carries in the fold of a garment meat sanctified as an acceptable offering to the Lord and the fold touches bread, soup, wine, oil, or any food, do they become sanctified? The priest answers "no," showing that something sanctified does not make something else sanctified by touching it. Haggai then asks the second question given by the Lord. If a person, defiled by contact with a corpse, touches bread, soup, wine, oil, or any food, do they become defiled? Following a decree of the Law found in the Book of Leviticus, which declares a person unclean who touches the corpse of a dead person (see Leviticus 22:4), and further declares that such uncleanliness is contagious, thus making anything touched by this unclean person defiled (see Leviticus 22:5), the priest must answer "yes."

The answers show sanctity is not passed on through physical touch, while defilement is. The Lord applies this law to the people, saying they defiled the offerings they made to the Lord because they were unclean in sinning against the Lord. Before the people lay one stone on top of the other in building the Temple, the Lord calls them to reflect on what occurred in the past. They never found as much as they expected. Instead of twenty ephahs (bushels) of wheat, there were only ten, and instead of fifty ephahs drawn from a vat, there were only twenty. Because of their defilement, the Lord struck them and all the work they did by searing wind, blight, and hail.

The Lord instructs the people to reflect from this day forward, from the twenty-fourth day of the ninth month (December 18, 520 BC), the date of the rebuilding of the foundation of the Temple. The Lord rhetorically asks if seed remains in the storehouse, or whether the vine, the fig, the pomegranate, and the olive tree have still borne fruit. From this day forward, the Lord will bless Judah with a fruitful harvest.

Haggai receives the Word of the Lord a second time on the twenty-fourth day of the month (December 18, 520 BC). The Lord directs Haggai to speak to Zerubbabel, informing the governor the Lord will shake heaven and earth and overthrow the thrones of kings and the power of the nations by causing their chariots and horses and all their riders to destroy each other in battle.

On the day the nations are overthrown, the Lord will choose Zerubbabel, the servant of the Lord, and make him like a signet ring, a chosen one of the Lord. A signet ring was a ring or some other instrument used as a seal to place an official mark on a document or some other material. In the Book of Jeremiah, the Lord, angered by the sins of Coniah (a shortened form of Jeconiah, the name Jeremiah gives King Jehoiachin,

Zerubbabel's grandfather), tells him that if he, "...were a signet ring on my right hand, I would snatch you off" (Jeremiah 22:24). The Lord's choice of Zerubbabel reverses the punishment cast on Coniah and his offspring.

Review Questions

1. Why did the Lord punish the people for not building the Temple?
2. What is the role of the governor among the people of Judah?
3. What is the significance of the message about the signet ring concerning Zerubbabel's role as governor?

Closing Prayer (SEE PAGE 15)

Pray the closing prayer now or after *lectio divina.*

Lectio Divina (SEE PAGE 8)

Relax your body and maintain a posture of prayer (back straight, eyes shut, feet flat on the floor). This exercise can take as long as you want, but in the context of this Bible study, 10 to 20 minutes should be sufficient.

The meditations that follow are provided only to help group participants use this prayer form, but note that lectio is intended to bring one to a place of prayerful contemplation where the Word of God speaks to the hearer from his or her heart. (See page 8 for further instruction.)

Response of the Leaders and People (1)

The Lord does not need our praise, but the Lord appreciates and glories in it. The Book of Haggai, as well as the other books in the Bible, stresses the Lord's pleasure in receiving praise from human beings. In the Gospel of Luke, we read about Jesus, the image of the invisible God, expressing disappointment after he healed ten lepers and only one returned to thank him. He asks, "Where are the other nine?" (Luke 17:17).

In the Book of Haggai, the Lord blesses the Jews when they rebuild the Temple. When we thank the Lord, perform good deeds for the love of God, or turn our heart to God in prayer, the Lord appreciates our gifts. Strange to say, we can do something God cannot do. Only we can give our love and our thanks to God. If God forced us to give love or thanks, it would no longer be our love or thanks, but God's.

✠ *What can I learn from this passage?*

Assurance of God's Presence (2)

When Jesus told his followers they were the light of the world, he meant people of the world would recognize they were followers of Christ (see Matthew 5:14–16). The Lord speaks of the people of Judah being like a signet ring. The signet ring is like a light pointing to the owner of the ring. By saying the people of Judah were a signet ring, the Lord was saying they were a light to the world, bringing glory to the Lord by their manner of acting. In this sense, all Christians who live according to the law of Christ live as a seal of Christ's presence in the world. They are the light of the world.

✠ *What can I learn from this passage?*

PART 2: INDIVIDUAL STUDY (ZECHARIAH 1—8)

Day 1: First Three Visions (Zechariah 1—2)

In the second year of Darius, in the eighth month (October–November 520 BC), the Word of the Lord came to Zechariah, the son of Berechiah, son of Iddo. In the Book of Nehemiah, the author speaks of someone named Zechariah as belonging to the priestly family of Iddo (see Nehemiah 12:16). Although Zechariah is identified as a prophet in this current book, the concept of him being a priest does not conflict with the idea he is also a prophet.

After the brief introduction of Zechariah, the editor abruptly turns to the message of Zechariah who speaks to the people of Judah about the Lord being angry with their ancestors. The Lord directs Zechariah to tell the people to return to the Lord and the Lord will return to them. Warning them not to be like their ancestors who refused to listen to the earlier prophets and turn from their deeds, the Lord asks where their ancestors were. The expression "earlier prophets" refers to those who prophesied before the Babylonians forced the Judeans into exile. The Judeans of Zechariah's day knew of the devastation and death of their people at the time of the Babylonian exile. Many of them died, many others were maimed, and many were weakened by disease and plague. Although the prophets died, their words caused a number of the Judeans to repent, realizing the Lord treated them as their sins deserved.

In the second year of Darius, on the twenty-fourth day of Shebat, the eleventh month (February 15, 519 BC), the Word of the Lord came to Zechariah in a vision. He was looking out at night when he spied a man mounted on a red horse in the shadows among myrtle trees, with red, sorrel, and white horses standing behind him. Zechariah asked what they were. Although the author does not mention men mounted on the red, sorrel, and white horses, the message continues as though each horse has a rider. The man standing among the myrtle trees said they were the ones sent by the Lord to patrol the earth. The riders answer the man standing among the myrtle trees, who is now identified as an angel of the Lord, saying they patrolled the earth and all rests quietly. When Darius I seized the throne, revolts erupted among the nations, but at this time, they had subsided.

The angel then asks the Lord of hosts how long the Lord would refuse to show mercy for Jerusalem and the cities of Judah, which endured the Lord's anger for seventy years. The seventy years refer to the seventy years the Lord would be angry with the Israelites (see Jeremiah 25:11 and 29:10). Zechariah views the seventy years as indicating the period of time the people would be without a temple in Jerusalem.

The angel proclaimed the Word of the Lord to Zechariah, saying the Lord is jealous for Jerusalem and Zion and has not become angry with the complacent nations who took advantage of the Babylonian invasion of Judah. Some of these nations ransacked Judah when it was severely destroyed and defenseless after the Babylonian conquest. The Lord was only a little angry, seeking light punishment for Judah at the hands of the enemy, but the invasions were so much more destructive, the Lord became angry with the invading nations.

The Lord returns to Jerusalem in a spirit of mercy, allowing the house of the Lord to be rebuilt in the city. A measuring line, a builder's string, will be extended over Jerusalem, symbolizing the reconstruction of the city. Zechariah is to proclaim that prosperity will overflow in the cities of Judah and the Lord will again bring comfort to Zion, again choosing Jerusalem for the Lord's house.

In his second vision, Zechariah sees four horns and asks the angel who spoke to him what they were. The angel responds these were the horns that scattered Judah, Israel, and Jerusalem. The four horns symbolized the might of Judah's enemies, most likely Assyria, Babylon, and Persia. The number four symbolizes the four points of the land: north, south, east, and west—in other words, every power on earth.

The Lord showed Zechariah four workmen, and the prophet asks what they are coming to do. The angel responds these workmen have come to terrify the nations (horns) that scattered Judah, scattering them as they scattered Judah. It was a custom to scatter some captives into exile in other lands where they would not be able to unify for a rebellion.

In a third vision, Zechariah sees a man with a measuring cord in his hand and asks him where he is going. The man replies he is going to measure the length and width of Jerusalem. Another angel comes into the vision and tells the angel who spoke to Zechariah to run and speak to that official, apparently the man with the measuring cord, telling him Jerusalem will not build a wall because of the large number of people and animals in its midst.

The Lord promises to be a wall of fire to protect Jerusalem, and the glory of the Lord will dwell in its midst. When the Israelites were traveling unprotected by a wall in their journey through the desert under Moses' leadership, the Lord preceded them at night by means of a column of fire (see Exodus 13:21). Although Jerusalem's walls would be built in the late fifth century, the newly growing nation could not foresee the enormity of its growth, leaving the size of the city not yet fully established. Another reason for not building a wall could be the need for caution against appearing to build fortifications for a rebellion against Persia.

The angel calls out to the people of Judah to flee from the land of the north, namely Babylon. When the Babylonians invaded Judah, some of the inhabitants found ample time to escape by fleeing to other nations. The angel speaks of the Lord dispersing the people of Judah to the four winds, meaning they fled in every direction or went into exile in Babylon. Speaking through the mediation of the angel, the Lord declares those who struck Judah struck the Lord of Judah and, as a result, the nations who plundered Judah will now be plundered by their own servants. The angel declares when this happens, Zechariah will know the Lord sent him.

The Lord rouses Zion to sing out in joy at the news the Lord God is in their midst. On that day, many nations will become followers of the Lord of Zion. These other nations will become a people of God, and the Lord will dwell in their midst, meaning the covenant the Lord made with Israel will now become a universal covenant for all people. The Lord will inherit Judah as the Lord's portion of the holy land. This is the first time "holy land" is used in the Bible. The Lord will again choose Jerusalem which was the Lord's city before the Babylonian invasion. The angel orders all the people to be silent as the Lord comes forth from the tabernacle.

Lectio Divina

Spend 8 to 10 minutes in silent contemplation of the following passage:

Although the people of Judah suffered in the darkness of exile for fifty years, the Lord showed mercy to the nation and still promised to reside in their midst in Jerusalem. Knowing the Lord is in their midst leads the people to sing and rejoice. The books of the prophets end with some form of promise of a new and better life for the nation, whether in the present or the future. This was a source of hope for the nation.

In the Gospels, Jesus never speaks of his passion and death without adding a message about his resurrection. The hope for resurrection encourages many suffering Christians to remain faithful to the Lord in the midst of turmoil. In the Scriptures, the light of hope is always there—at the end of the tunnel.

✠ *What can I learn from this passage?*

Day 2: Prophetic Vision (Zechariah 3)

In a fourth vision, Zechariah sees Joshua, the high priest, standing before the angel of the Lord, while an adversary stands at Joshua's right to accuse him. "Adversary" in Hebrew means "Satan," who is portrayed not as an evil opponent, but as a type of prosecuting attorney in the Lord's heavenly courtroom. This image of Satan as a prosecuting attorney is not unique to this book. In the Book of Job, Satan is also portrayed as a type of prosecuting attorney in the heavenly court where he challenges the Lord to take away Job's gifts to test Job (see Job 1:6–12).

An angel of the Lord addresses the adversary, asking the Lord—who has chosen Jerusalem as the holy city—to rebuke the adversary. Joshua is special to the Lord, like a brand plucked from a fire. Since he is clothed in filthy garments, the angel instructed those with him to remove the filthy garments. The angel of the Lord informed Joshua he removed guilt from him with his garments and will replace them with fine garments. The angel ordered those with him to put a clean turban on Joshua's head and clothe him in festive apparel in the presence of the Lord. The garments are those belonging to the priestly office.

The angel then tells Joshua the Lord has chosen him to fulfill the priestly duties. He is to remain faithful to the laws of the Lord and teach them to the people, fulfill the rituals, administer the laborers and lands of the Temple domain, and participate in the Lord's judicial courts in difficult cases. The Lord will give him access to the heavenly realm.

The Lord instructs Joshua and his associates to listen to the Word of the Lord. Joshua and his associates, symbolizing the restored priesthood, are signs of things to come. The Lord will restore the Davidic line, symbolized as the Branch. Zerubbabel could already be a sign of the restored Davidic line, although he is only a governor and not a king.

The Lord placed before Joshua a stone with seven facets. The stone represents the precious stones adorning the high priest's clothing. The seven facets (eyes) indicate the totality of their role as instruments of God's vigilance and action. The Lord will engrave an inscription on the stone and, in one day, will take away the guilt of the people. On that day, the priests will invite each other to rest peacefully under their vines and fig trees.

Lectio Divina

Spend 8 to 10 minutes in silent contemplation of the following passage:

Later in the Scriptures, the adversary, Satan, will become an adversary against God and goodness. The role of the adversary in Zechariah depicts the ancient idea of testing a person to prove one's worth. It is not done for evil purposes, but to prove the faithfulness of the Lord's servants. In the Book of Wisdom, we read about those called to share in the glory of the Lord: "Chastised a little, they shall be greatly blessed, because God tried them and found them worthy ..." (Wisdom 3:5). Those who remained faithful to the Lord have proven their worthiness to share in the Lord's eternal salvation.

✠ *What can I learn from this passage?*

Day 3: The Last Three Visions (Zechariah 4—6)

The angel who had been speaking to Zechariah in the past roused him as though from sleep and asked him what he saw. He responded he saw a golden lamp stand with a bowl on top of it. In it were seven lamps with seven spouts on the top of each of the lamps. On each side of the lamp stand he saw an olive tree. The lamp stand represents the usual furnishings in the Temple. The two olive trees could symbolize prosperity and permanence, or Joshua the high priest and Zerubbabel the governor, two just leaders who symbolize the human foundation of Judah. When the angel asks Zechariah if he knows what these things are, Zechariah answers, "No."

Following the question is an oracle which appears to be a later insertion, since it does not follow the opening passage of chapter 4. The Lord says to Zechariah the Word of the Lord for Zerubbabel is: "Not by might, and not by power, but by my spirit" (4:6). The mountain becomes a plain before Zerubbabel, meaning the land is being prepared for the building of the Temple. Zerubbabel will bring the first stone amid the shouts of the people proclaiming favor on it, and he will finish the building of the Temple. The first stone is the foundation stone which was often laid among great shouting and ritual festivities. When this happens, Zechariah will know the Lord sent the angel to him. Whoever looked with mockery on the day of such a small beginning will rejoice to see the capstone, the finishing stone, in the hand of Zerubbabel.

The seven spouts on the lamp stand are like small openings that the angel declares are the seven eyes of the Lord that range over the whole world. Zechariah then asks what the two olive trees are and the two streams from the olive tree that pour out golden oil through two gold taps. The angel answers they are the two anointed ones who stand by the Lord of the whole earth. Since the leader and high priest are not the anointed ones, the image seems to indicate their positions in the idealized restored nation. Just as Moses (leader) and Aaron (priesthood) represented the leadership of the Israelites in the past, so the governor and high priest of the restored nation follow in this tradition.

In chapter 5, Zechariah experiences a fifth vision of a flying scroll. The angel who spoke to him asked what he saw, and he said he saw a flying scroll twenty cubits long and ten cubits wide (29 feet by 15 feet). This would be a very large flying scroll, but it fits in perfectly with the entryway to the Temple. The flying scroll will travel over the whole land, bringing a curse to every thief and those who swear falsely by the name of the Lord. It shall lodge itself in the house of the thief and perjurer, consuming the house, timber, and stones alike.

In the sixth vision, Zechariah asks the angel what he is seeing, and the angel tells him it is the basket that is coming, representing all the wickedness in the land. When the lead cover of the basket is lifted, Zechariah sees a woman sitting inside it. The angel says the woman is wickedness, and he throws her inside the basket and pushes the lead weight into its opening.

Zechariah raises his eyes up and sees two women approaching, with the wind under their wings which appears to be the wings of a stork. When they lift the basket into the air, Zechariah asks where they are taking it. The angel answers they are taking it to the land of Shinar in Babylon, where they would build a temple for it and, when the temple is finished, they will set it there on its base. Placing the basket on its base means it is placed where people once worshiped false gods. Moving the basket from Judah to Babylon alludes to sending all the false gods back to Babylon. Some of the exiles coming from Babylon may have brought with them the worship of Babylonian idols.

In chapter 6, Zechariah experiences his seventh vision, consisting of four chariots coming out from between two mountains made of bronze. The group of strong horses pulling the chariots were each a different color, red, black, white, and dappled. When Zechariah asked what these were, the angel said these were the four winds of the heavens, coming forth after presenting themselves before the Lord of all the earth. The angel said the chariot with the black horses was going toward the land of the north, the one with the white horses was going toward the west, and the one with the dappled horses was going toward the land of the south. These strong horses were restless to set out to patrol the earth. The angel cried out to Zechariah that those who go to the land of the north provide rest for the spirit of the Lord. Because the land of the north is being punished for its wickedness, the spirit of the Lord is able to rest.

The Word of the Lord came to the angel, directing him to take silver and gold from the exiles Heldai, Tobijah, Jedaiah, who arrived from exile in Babylon. The angel is to make crowns with these precious metals and the same day is to go to the house of Josiah, son of Zephaniah. The text becomes confusing at this point, perhaps due to some of the text being lost.

At the house of Josiah, the text says, the angel is to place a crown on the head of Joshua, son of Jehozadak, the high priest. Zerubbabel should be the one crowned, however. The angel, proclaiming the Word of the Lord, says there is a man whose name is Branch. Although Zerubbabel has been mentioned previously as the governor and the one responsible for building the Temple and the one who is apparently referred to as the "Branch," he is missing totally from this scene of crowning. From the following text, we can conclude Zerubbabel was crowned since he was the one who built the Temple.

Zerubbabel, the Branch, will branch out and build the Temple of the Lord. When the text relates he will take up the royal insignia and sit as a ruler on his throne, it adds the priest will sit on his right hand. Joshua is the high priest. Peace will exist between the two of them, Zerubbabel and Joshua, who accept each other's specific role in the restored Jerusalem.

The other crown will be placed in the Temple of the Lord as a reminder to Heldai, Tobijah, Jedaiah, and the son of Zephaniah (Josiah). People from far away will come and build the Temple of the Lord. When Zechariah observes this, he will know the Lord of hosts sent the angel. All this will take place if the people truly obey the Lord their God.

Lectio Divina

Spend 8 to 10 minutes in silent contemplation of the following passage:

> Jesus said, "I have come to set the earth on fire, and how I wish it were already blazing!" (Luke 12:49). We would be happy to live in a world where everyone loved God and each other as Jesus asked. This is the fire Jesus would like to see blazing across the world, a fire of love. How happy we would be in a world burning with love. The fact is the Lord would be equally happy with such a creation. In Zechariah, the Lord has cleared away wickedness from Judah and sees the end of wicked Babylon. Zechariah speaks of this scenario as bringing rest to the spirit of the Lord. We should love one another because God wills it, and we should love one another because God rejoices in it.

✠ *What can I learn from this passage?*

Day 4: Judah and Zion Restored (Zechariah 7—8)

In the fourth year of King Darius of Persia, the Word of the Lord came to Zechariah on the fourth day of the ninth month (December 7, 518 BC). Since the Temple was now being rebuilt, some men ask the priests of the Temple whether they should continue the practice of weeping and abstaining on the fifth month as was done in the past. The Israelites set aside the fifth month to mourn over the destruction of the Temple, which took place in 587 BC. The priests were the ones who made judgments concerning the observance of memorials.

Although the men asked only about fasting and weeping in the fifth month, the Lord, in response, speaks of the fasting and mourning in the fifth and seventh month. The fasting and mourning in the seventh month was in memory of Gedaliah, a king of Judah appointed by the king of Babylon after the destruction of Jerusalem. The people of Judah accepted Gedaliah as their king, but Ishmael, a descendant of the royal line of the House of David, wanted to be king, so he assassinated Gedaliah in the seventh month (see 2 Kings 25:22–26).

The Lord asks the people if their mourning and fasting from eating and drinking in the fifth and seventh month was for the Lord or for themselves. Although they mourned and fasted at these times, the people ignored the other demands of the law of the Lord by their selfishness and sinfulness, causing the Lord to unleash the Babylonians on Judah and Jerusalem.

The Word of the Lord comes to Zechariah, urging him to remind the people of their past sins and the warnings the Lord sent them through the mouths of the earlier prophets, when Jerusalem and the surrounding cities were inhabited and secure. In the past, the Lord instructed them to judge with proper justice, exhibiting kindness and compassion to each other. They were not to oppress the widow, the orphan, the resident alien, or the poor, and they were not to plot evil against one another.

Despite the Lord's many warnings, the people of Jerusalem and Judah refused to listen to the Lord, turning their back on the Lord and covering their ears so they would not hear. They made their heart as hard as diamonds and rejected the Word of the Lord they received from the prophets. As a result, the Lord became furious and punished them, using the tactics they used. Just as they refused to listen to the Lord when the Lord called out to them, so the Lord would not listen to them when they cried out to the Lord. As punishment, the Lord scattered them among foreign nations, leaving the once-pleasant land of Judah desolate.

Chapter 8 begins with seven oracles concerning the restoration of Judah and Zion followed by three oracles concerning Judah's relationship with other nations. The chapter makes no mention of Zechariah, beginning simply with the words, "Then the Word of the LORD of hosts came."

The first oracle speaks of the Lord's jealousy for Zion, meaning the

Lord's special favor for the city of Jerusalem and the people of Judah. The second oracle declares the Lord has returned to Zion and will dwell in Jerusalem, the faithful city. Jerusalem is the mountain of the Lord of hosts, the holy mountain, which is a reference to the city and the Temple.

The third oracle speaks of a peaceful community, declaring old men and women will sit in the streets of Jerusalem with a staff in their hands. Joy will be heard again in the sound of children playing in the streets.

The fourth oracle speaks of the power of the Lord. Even if the restoration would seem impossible to the remnant of the people, it should not be seen as impossible for the Lord. It also speaks of the Lord's plan to rescue the people from the land of the rising sun to the land of the setting sun, from east to west. The Lord will lead them back to Jerusalem, and they will be God's people and the Lord will be their God, in faithfulness and justice.

In the fifth oracle, the Lord tells the people to let their hands be strong. The people are those who heard the words spoken through the prophets when the foundation of the Temple was laid. In the past, there were no wages for the workers, no one able to hire animals, no safety against the enemy for travelers since the Lord set one against the other. The Lord will no longer treat the remnant in the same manner.

The oracle speaks of a sowing of peace, meaning the people will live with peace planted in the land. The vine will produce its fruit, the land its crops, and the heavens dew. The Lord will provide all this for the remnant. Just as Judah and Israel were a curse among the nations, so now the Lord will save them so they will become a blessing. The Lord tells them not to fear but to be strong.

In the seventh oracle, the Lord recalls the period when the people were punished because they angered the Lord their God. The Lord did not relent then, but now the Lord plans to favor Jerusalem and Judah, telling them to abandon fear. They must speak truthfully to one another and render honest and complete justice at the gates. When the people had a grievance to settle, the elders would sit at the gates as judges. They must not plot against each other, or swear a false oath. The Lord truly hates these evils.

In the first of the three oracles concerning Judah and the nations, the Lord declares the fourth, fifth, seventh, and tenth months which were times for mourning will now become occasions of joy and gladness, and cheerful festivals for the house of Judah. Added to the days of mourning found in 7:3–5 (in the fifth and seventh month), the oracle adds two more, namely the fourth and the tenth months. The fourth month commemorates the departure of the leaders of Judah from Jerusalem (see 2 Kings 25:3–7), and the tenth month marks the beginning of the siege of Jerusalem (see 2 Kings 25:1). This oracle answers the question of continued fasting and weeping (mourning) while the Temple was being built (see 7:3).

The second oracle declares people and inhabitants of many cities will come, with the inhabitants of one city urging those of the others to join them in seeking the favor of the Lord of hosts. Many people and strong nations will come to Jerusalem to seek the Lord and the favor of the Lord. The third oracle speaks of ten people from nations of every language taking hold of the cloak of every Jew and asking to go with them, because they heard God is with them.

Lectio Divina

Spend 8 to 10 minutes in silent contemplation of the following passage:

> The impossible becomes possible with the Lord. Judah, victimized and devastated by the onslaught of powerful nations, becomes a favored nation, with other nations streaming toward it with gifts and support. The Lord brings Judah from desolation to prosperity. In Mark's Gospel, Jesus heals a boy with a demon and says, "Everything is possible to one who has faith" (Mark 9:23). Human beings can bring about miraculous changes in the world if they have faith.

✠ *What can I learn from this passage?*

Review Questions

1. What was the message of the first vision Zechariah received?
2. What was the message of the second vision Zechariah received?
3. What was the message of the third vision Zechariah received?
4. What are the duties of Joshua, the high priest?

The Books of Zechariah (II) and Malachi

ZECHARIAH 9–14 AND MALACHI

I will refine them as one refines silver, and I will test them as one tests gold. They will call upon my name, and I will answer them; I will say, "They are my people," and they will say, "The LORD is my God" (Zechariah 13:9).

Opening Prayer (SEE PAGE 15)

Context

Part 1: Zechariah 9—11:3 When the editors of Second Zechariah wrote, they used many of the words and thoughts of earlier prophets to construct a variety of literary forms in their writing. Second Zechariah contains parables, poems, narratives, and prophetic messages from the Lord, inserted in the book by later editors. It strives to keep alive the hope for a revival of Jerusalem and the Temple. Chapters 9 and 10 speak of the restoration of the land and the people of Judah, but this section ends with the first three verses of chapter 11, a prelude to what is described as "The Shepherd Narrative."

Part 2: Zechariah 11:4—14 The Lord reviles the worthless and evil shepherds and promises to protect Judah against the nations that once oppressed her. Besides rejecting the worthless shepherds, the Lord also rejects the false prophets and promises to destroy them and their idols. In the end, the enemies of Jerusalem will be destroyed and Jerusalem will become a nation holy to the Lord.

Malachi After the people's return from exile, many become complacent and ignore the law of the Lord, believing nothing is gained by remaining faithful to the Lord. The Lord condemns their sinfulness and warns about their impending destruction if they do not repent.

PART 1: GROUP STUDY (ZECHARIAH 9—11:3)

Read aloud Zechariah 9—11:3.

9 Restoration of the Land of Israel

An oracle of the Lord, spoken through the prophet Zechariah, names the nations surrounding the land of Israel and cries out against them. Tyre became strong, rich in precious silver and gold, as abundant as dust and mud in the streets. Despite its wealth and strength, the Lord will disinherit the nation, casting their wealth into the sea or devouring it with fire. Other nations will view the devastation and shiver in fear and anguish. The king of the nation will disappear and their land will be uninhabited.

The pride of the Philistines will meet with destruction, with the Lord tearing their idolatry from their mouths and their sacrifices from between their teeth. They will become only a remnant before the Lord, living as though one of the clans of Judah, no longer a great nation. They will be like the Jebusites who inhabited Jerusalem before David conquered the land and who were eventually absorbed into Judah's culture. The presence of the Lord in the house of the Lord, the Temple, will be like a garrison against invaders. Now that the Lord has witnessed the affliction of the people of Judah, the Lord will no longer allow any oppressor to again overwhelm them. The Lord's powerful presence among the people links the message of Second Zechariah with that of First Zechariah.

Addressing the people with the affectionate name of "daughter Jerusalem," the Lord invites Zion to express the joy of the people with a loud voice. The prophet reports the Lord's word to the people, inviting them to behold their king coming to them as a just savior, humbly riding on a donkey, a colt which is the foal of a donkey. The image of a king coming on a donkey instead of a horse shows the king comes in peace and not for battle. In speaking of a donkey, a colt, the prophet makes use of a Hebrew practice of using parallelisms to enforce an image. The text is actually speaking of a single animal. In Matthew's Gospel, the author applies this text to Jesus' triumphal entry into Jerusalem and interprets the naming of the colt as though it were distinct from the donkey, thus quoting the prophecy and saying the king (Jesus) comes "riding on an ass, and on a colt, the foal of a beast of burden" (Matthew 21:5–7).

The king who comes in peace will not come with the weapons of an army, symbolized by the chariot, horse, and bow, but will proclaim peace to the nations. The king shall rule from sea to sea, from the river (Euphrates) to the ends of the earth.

The Lord remained faithful to the blood of the covenant, a reference to the sacrifices which sealed the covenant. The Lord freed the prisoners, the exiles, from a waterless pit. The Lord calls the exiles to return to the fortress, meaning the protection of the Lord in Jerusalem. The Lord makes Judah as powerful as the Lord's bow, using the exiles from Ephraim (the destroyed northern kingdom of Israel) as the Lord's arrows.

The sons of Zion will battle against the Greeks (Yavan) with the Lord guiding their arrows to shoot as swift as lightning. The Lord will sound the ram's horn for battle and arrive in a storm from the south. Protected by the Lord, the people of Judah will devour and conquer the enemy with slingshots filled with stones, which recalls the story of David, who slew the giant Goliath with a sling and a stone (see 1 Samuel 17:49).

In victory, the people of Zion will celebrate with wine and full bowls of food, like the offerings left at the corners of the altar in the Temple that were always filled. The Lord will save them as though they were the Lord's flock. Like precious stones in a crown, they will shine in grandeur and beauty over the land. Grain and wine will provide an abundant feast for the men and women.

10—11:3 Blessings on Judah and Ephraim

In chapter 10, the prophet tells the people to ask the Lord, who brings storm clouds and heavy rains, to grant rain during the spring season to provide grain in the fields. The devious diviners spoke of false visions that provided deceitful and empty comfort. The people of Judah were like sheep without a shepherd, wandering about aimlessly. The Lord will punish the leaders of the people who had the duty of shepherding the flock.

Unlike these false leaders, the Lord of hosts attends to the flock, the house of Judah, making them like a splendid horse in battle. From Judah will come every need for battle, a tower, tent pegs, bows and arrows, and officers. Marching as one, the people of Judah will be like warriors who trample over muddy streets in battle, waging war with the companionship of the Lord, and shaming the enemy's horses. The Lord will save the house of Judah (the people of the southern kingdom) and the house of Joseph (the exiles from the northern kingdom).

With deep compassion, the Lord their God, acting as though they were never cast off, will call them to change their life and return to the Lord. The once defeated Ephraim (the people of the northern kingdom) will be like a hero, enriched with wine, and blessed with children who will rejoice and exult in the Lord. The people of the northern kingdom will become one with Judah. Like a shepherd, the Lord will whistle and gather the Israelites in, redeeming them and making them as numerous as they had been before. The Lord planted them like a farmer who sowed them among distant nations, where they remained faithful to the Lord, bore children, and left to return to their homeland.

During the invasion of the Babylonians, many of the inhabitants of Judah settled in exile in Egypt, and many of the Israelites of the northern kingdom were forced to settle in exile in Assyria. Egypt and Assyria at one time supported the Israelites in battle, but they eventually became their oppressors. The Lord will bring the Israelites back to the Promised Land. They will settle in Lebanon and Gilead, two areas of the original Promised Land, and their numbers will become so great there will scarcely be any room for them. The Lord will destroy Egypt, dry up the Nile River, and demolish Assyria. The Lord, in whose name they live, will strengthen them.

At the beginning of chapter 11, the Lord calls upon Lebanon to open its doors to the Day of Judgment, when fire will devour its cedars. Using a poetic image, the prophet speaks of the destruction of the cypress trees and cedar trees to refer to the destruction of the nation. The prophet further speaks of the cypress trees and oaks of Bashan wailing because the great forests have been devoured, a poetic reference to the destruction of that nation. The evil shepherds of Israel wail at the loss of power and glory. "Shepherds" could be a reference to the kings or the prophets who did not fulfill their ministry in shepherding the flock, namely the people of Israel. The young lions (the leaders) roar over the destruction of the lush valley of the Jordan.

Review Questions

1. What is the meaning of Zechariah's message concerning a king who will come to the people of Jerusalem riding on a donkey? How is this message applied in Matthew's Gospel?
2. Who are the leaders of the people and why is the Lord displeased with them?
3. Why is the Lord so concerned about Ephraim?

Closing Prayer (SEE PAGE 15)

Pray the closing prayer now or after *lectio divina*.

Lectio Divina (SEE PAGE 8)

Relax your body and maintain a posture of prayer (back straight, eyes shut, feet flat on the floor). This exercise can take as long as you want, but in the context of this Bible study, 10 to 20 minutes should be sufficient.

The meditations that follow are provided only to help group participants use this prayer form, but note that lectio is intended to bring one to a place of prayerful contemplation where the Word of God speaks to the hearer from his or her heart. (See page 8 for further instruction.)

Restoration of the Land of Israel (9)

The Lord reminds us that conquests do not demand a powerful army but a spirit of humble dedication to one's mission. In this passage, the Lord speaks of a great king coming to the people riding on a humble donkey rather than a majestic stallion ready for battle (9:9). Matthew quotes from this text when describing the triumphant entry of Jesus, the king of peace, riding on a humble donkey (see Matthew 21:5). The New Testament often portrays humility and weakness as a powerful weapon in the world. Jesus, who is God, came as a humble human being; he was captured, scourged, and killed, yet he changed the direction of history. Paul, the Apostle to the Gentiles, boasts of his weakness, saying, "Therefore, I am content with weaknesses, insults, hardships, persecutions, and constraints, for the sake of Christ; for when I am weak, then I am strong" (2 Corinthians 12:10). From the example of the willingness of Jesus and Paul to suffer, we learn the power of suffering in changing the world.

✠ *What can I learn from this passage?*

Blessings on Judah and Ephraim (10—11:3)

The Lord promises to bless the people of Judah with an abundance of grain and wine, but the people must pray for these gifts. The Lord tells them to ask for rain in the spring season and, if they do so, they will receive the heavy rains needed for an abundant crop. The need for prayer to obtain God's blessings echoes through the ages to the time of Jesus who said, "Ask and it will be given to you; seek and you will find; knock and the door will be opened to you" (Matthew 7:7). Prayer is basic to the life of all who believe in God. When we pray, God may not give us what we want, but God responds by giving us what we need.

✠ *What can I learn from this passage?*

PART 2: INDIVIDUAL STUDY (ZECHARIAH 11:4—14 AND MALACHI)

Day 1: Oracles Concerning the Nations and Judah (Zechariah 11:4—12)

The Lord commissions Zechariah to work as a shepherd for the people who are about to be slaughtered. In an allegory, the prophet pictures the people like sheep who are bought and sold. Like sheep, they are sold to the conquerors, who can slaughter them as they wish with no retribution. Those who sell them become rich, an apparent reference to the evil leaders who profit by betraying their own people. The Lord will reject the buyers and sellers, delivering them into each other's power or to the power of their own leaders. The oppressors shall ravage the land and the Lord will do nothing to protect it.

Zechariah acted out the prophecy given by the Lord by accepting the role of a shepherd for the merchants, namely those who betray the people. He took two staffs, one named Delight and the other Union. Delight refers to the Mosaic covenant, and Union refers to the unity between the tribes of the northern kingdom of Israel and the southern kingdom of Judah. He shepherded the flock (nation) and claimed to do away with three shepherds. The reference to the three shepherds is unclear; it may refer to wicked kings or false prophets. When the nation exhausted Zechariah's patience and despised him, he refused to be their shepherd, leaving the wicked to their fate, not caring whether they died or were killed. He added in frustration those who remain will then demolish each other.

Zechariah took the staff named Delight and snapped it in two, breaking the covenant he made with the people when he agreed to shepherd them. Those who betrayed the people understood Zechariah's actions as a message from the Lord. Zechariah asked them for his wages if it seemed good to them, otherwise they should withhold them. They counted out thirty pieces of silver, which, according to the Book of Exodus 21:32, is the price owed to an owner of a slave gored by another man's ox. Zechariah threw the thirty pieces of silver into the Temple treasury, as directed by the Lord, to show the contempt the people had for the Lord, paying only the price of an injured slave to the Lord.

Zechariah then snapped the second staff called Union in two, symbolically breaking the unity between Judah and Israel. The Lord then commissioned Zechariah to work as a shepherd for the people, but this time to be like the wicked shepherds who fatten themselves on the flesh of the sheep, even tearing off their hooves (shoes), not caring that some of the sheep disappeared, strayed, needed healing or food. The Lord will curse the worthless shepherd who forsakes the flock, slicing his arm or his right eye with a sword, causing the arm to wither and his eye to be blind.

Chapter 12 begins with an oracle of the Lord concerning the Lord's protection of the people. The almighty Lord, who spread out the heavens, laid the foundations of the earth, and fashioned the human spirit, reveals the protection given to Jerusalem and Judah. The Lord will make Jerusalem like a cup of reeling for all the surrounding nations, which means it will be like a cup of liquor causing the nations to stumble like intoxicated people. Judah and Jerusalem will be invaded and protected. The Lord will make Jerusalem like a heavy stone causing those who attempt to lift it to be injured, even if all the invaders join together in the siege.

The Lord declares on that day, the Lord will watch over the people of Judah, blinding all the horses of the invaders and causing horses and riders to panic. The people of Judah will praise the strength of the Lord as shown in Jerusalem. The clans of Judah will be like a brazier of fire in the woods and like a burning torch among sheaves that will devour all the surrounding nations, while Jerusalem itself will remain safe.

The Lord expresses the intention of saving the tents of Judah first, before Jerusalem. With the devastation of Judah by the Babylonians and the return of the people to a devastated land, many of the people had to live in tents. By saving the tents of Judah first, the Lord avoids the appearance of the house of David (the king) and Jerusalem being favored over all Judah. On that day, the Lord will shield all of Jerusalem to the point the weakest will have the strength of David and the house of David (the king) will be like God, like the angel of the Lord shielding the people. When the author says the people of Jerusalem will be like God, he is not speaking of people being like the Lord but is using the term to mean people with unbeatable strength.

On that day, the Lord intends to destroy all the nations warring against Jerusalem. The Lord "will pour out on the house of David and the inhabitants of Jerusalem a spirit of mercy and supplication, so that when they look on him whom they have thrust through, they will mourn for him as one mourns for an only child, and they will grieve for him as one grieves over a firstborn" (12:10). It is unclear who is indicated by the one "whom they have thrust through," but this could refer to a descendant of David, a priestly leader, or even a prophet. The author of John's Gospel applies the text to the piercing of Christ's side after his death (see John 19:37). Grieving for the one who is thrust through will be as great as grieving for the loss of a firstborn, the child of the inheritance.

On that day, the mourning in Jerusalem shall be as great as the mourning of the Syrians when they grieve the death of the fertility god, Hadadrimmon, in the plain of Megiddo. At the end of the season for harvesting, the people annually mourned the death of their god. Every family in Jerusalem, the family of David, the family of Nathan, the family of Levi, the family of Shemei, and all the families with their women will mourn over the one who is thrust through. Nathan may be referring to one of the sons of David or to the prophet Nathan. Shemei is a grandson of Levi.

Lectio Divina

Spend 8 to 10 minutes in silent contemplation of the following passage:

Although we are not sure to whom Zechariah is referring when he speaks of "him whom they have thrust through," the application of the text to Jesus' death is helpful for Christians. Just as grieving follows the death of the Old Testament person, whoever he may be, so grieving follows in the New Testament when the evangelist John applies the text to Jesus (see John 19:37). Christians see Jesus on the cross and grieve over the atrocities that ended his life on earth, but they also see hope for the future. Salvation is achieved through Jesus' death, resurrection, ascension, and bestowing of the Holy Spirit. Because of Christ's resurrection, a Christian lives with hope, believing that following the grief of death is the glory of resurrection. According to the prophets, God leads the people through the darkness of their exile to a glorious new life in the Promised Land.

✠ *What can I learn from this passage?*

___

Day 2: Jerusalem Restored (Zechariah 13—14)

The prophet declares a fountain will be opened to purify the house of David and Jerusalem from sin and uncleanliness. It will be a day of cleansing, when idols and all uncleanliness will be removed from the land, and if any dare to prophecy, their parents will kill them with the sword because they lied in the Lord's name. The author is speaking of false prophets in this passage. On that day, the prophets will bow down in shame because of the false visions they prophesied and will not put on the hairy cloak that prophets wore. In the days of Elijah, some who met him described him as wearing "a hairy garment with a leather belt around his waist" (2 Kings 1:8).

The prophet orders the false prophets to declare they are not prophets. Since it was a custom for false prophets of Baal to lacerate themselves during worship of a false god, they could be identified by the wounds on their chest. The prophet of the Lord states if people asked the repentant false prophets the source of the wounds on their chest, they are to answer they received the wounds in the house of a friend.

An abrupt change takes place in the text as the prophet speaks of awaking the sword against the shepherd, portrayed as an associate of the Lord. The passage is not clear, since the shepherd could refer to those chosen to lead armies against Judah or those chosen to lead the people of Judah. The poem speaks of striking the shepherd, causing the sheep to scatter. With the destruction of the leader of the people, the people will be unprotected, living in chaos.

The prophet says the Lord will reject the little ones, an apparent reference to the people of Judah. Two-thirds of the people will be destroyed, and one-third will be left. The Lord will bring the one-third, the remnant, through fire to be refined and tested as silver and gold are tested. In the midst of their suffering, the remnant will turn back to the Lord. The Lord will declare they are the Lord's people, and they will profess the Lord is their God.

In chapter 14, Zechariah speaks in apocalyptic images of the day of the coming of the Lord. On that day, the Lord will gather together all the

___

nations against Jerusalem. The prophet describes the usual consequences of a battle, a city destroyed, women raped, and half of the inhabitants exiled, leaving the rest remaining in the city. Like a great warrior, the Lord will enter the battle, standing on the Mount of Olives, which is east of Jerusalem. Under the feet of the Lord, the Mount of Olives will be split in two by a very deep valley, cutting the mountain in half so that one half will move to the north, and the other to the south, with the valley going from east to west as far as Azal. Azal is not identified.

When the mountain splits, the people of Judah will flee as they did during an earthquake in the time of Uzziah, the king of Judah. In the Book of Amos, the author dates his writing as taking place "two years before the earthquake," when King Uzziah was king of Judah (see Amos 1:1). The earthquake left a lasting impression on the people of Judah. When the splitting of the mountain takes place, the Lord will come with all the holy ones, a reference to the heavenly army assisting the Lord.

The apocalyptic imagery continues as Zechariah speaks of the time when there will be one continuous day, neither cold nor frost, night nor day, but only light. In summer and winter, refreshing water will flow from Jerusalem, half to the eastern sea (the Dead Sea) and half to the western sea (the Mediterranean). This refreshing water will come from Jerusalem, thus symbolizing the Lord is king over all the earth. Jerusalem is no longer the city of the Davidic King but where the *Lord* is king. The Lord's name will be the only name of a deity. All the land from the northern border (Geba) to the southern border (Rimmon) will turn into a plain, with Jerusalem being exalted over all. The boundaries of Jerusalem will stretch over a vast area, from the Gate of Benjamin to the older first gate, from the Corner Gate and from the Tower of Hananel to the king's wine presses. Jerusalem shall become inhabited, never again threatened, instead a secure city.

The Lord will strike out against Jerusalem's enemies. The prophet describes a plague that will afflict those who battled against Jerusalem, making their flesh, their eyes, and their tongues rot. On that day, people will panic in confusion, fighting against each other. Judah will even fight against Jerusalem. The abundant riches of the nations will be seized, all their silver, gold, and garments. The horses, mules, camels, donkeys, and all animals in the camps will endure the same plague afflicting human beings.

The prophet declares all the people who once battled against Jerusalem and who survived the plague will come year after year to pay homage to the king, the Lord of hosts, to celebrate the feast of Booths. The feast of Booths refers to a harvest feast that was held in such high esteem the people referred to it as "the feast." The Lord will withhold rain from those who do not go to Jerusalem to pay homage. If the family of Egypt does not go to Jerusalem to pay homage, they will suffer the same plague endured by those who refuse to go to celebrate the feast of Booths. Egypt and all nations not going up to celebrate the feast of Booths will be punished in this manner.

The phrase "Holy to the Lord" will be inscribed on the horses' bells. Horses prepared for war wear bells as ornamentation. The priests often wore inscribed bells on their garments. By inscribing the term "Holy to the Lord" on the bells made them holy for battle in the end time. The horses are horses of peace, not of war. The pots used for refuse in the house of the Lord and every pot of the people in Jerusalem and Judah will become as holy to the Lord as the vessels before the altar so those who offer sacrifice may use them to cook the flesh offered in sacrifice. The day shall be so holy that merchants will no longer be found in the house of the Lord.

Lectio Divina

Spend 8 to 10 minutes in silent contemplation of the following passage:

In Matthew's Gospel, Jesus quotes from the Book of Zechariah, warning his disciples their faith will be shaken, saying, "I will strike the shepherd, and the sheep of the flock will be dispersed" (Matthew 26:31). Jesus is the good shepherd and Jesus' disciples are the sheep. Ironically, it is the striking of the Good Shepherd that led to our salvation and enabled Christians to be willing to suffer and die for Christ. Paul the Apostle writes: "But may I never boast except in the cross of our Lord Jesus Christ, through which the world has been crucified to me, and I to the world" (Galatians 6:14). Jesus' willingness to suffer and die for the flock did not disperse the flock throughout history but brought them together and greatly influenced the history of the world.

✠ *What can I learn from this passage?*

Day 3: Improper Worship (Malachi 1—2:9)

The Word of the Lord comes to Israel through Malachi. Malachi may be the name of some unknown prophet, but it could instead mean "my messenger" in Hebrew. The author wrote the Book of Malachi shortly after the Israelites returned to their homeland after their exile in Babylon.

When the Lord tells the descendants of Jacob, "I love you," the people ask how the Lord loves them. The Lord responds, recalling Esau, who was a brother of Jacob and had the right to the blessing given by Isaac, was rejected in favor of Jacob. Since that time, the Lord punished Edom, the descendants of Esau, by making the nation's mountains desolate and his territory a desert for wild beasts. The Lord declares even if Edom attempted to rebuild, the rebuilding would be torn down. The nation of Edom shall be known as the territory of wickedness, a witness to the Lord's lasting anger. The offspring of Jacob, namely Israel, shall see the greatness of the Lord proclaimed, even beyond the territory of Israel.

Knowing a son honors his father and a servant shows respect for his master, the Lord asks, as a father to the nation, where the honor due to him is shown, or as a master, where the reverence is that is due to him.

The Lord addresses the priests, accusing them of contempt for the name of the Lord, and they ask how they showed contempt for the Lord's name. The Lord says they offered defiled food on the altar of the Lord. They ask when they offered defiled food, and the Lord answers the table of the Lord is defiled when they offer a blind animal for sacrifice. The Lord asks whether they see any wrong in that or in offering a lame or sick animal in sacrifice. The priests should be familiar with the law as found in Leviticus, which declares: "You shall not offer one that has any blemish, for such a one would not be acceptable on your behalf" (Leviticus 22:20). The Lord challenges the audacity of the priests by asking if their governor would be pleased with their offering and as a result show them favor.

The prophet intrudes on the Word of the Lord with his own comment, urging the people to implore God's favor to receive mercy from the Lord. He questions whether the Lord should show them any mercy since they have acted in such a vile manner.

The prophet returns to sharing the Word of the Lord with the people. In frustration with the offerings, the Lord wishes one of the priests would shut the Temple gates to keep out the wicked sacrifices burnt on the Lord's altar. The Lord of hosts takes no pleasure in those who make these offerings and refuses to accept them.

In contrast to the defiled offering of the priests of Judah, the Lord declares from the rising of the sun (east) to its setting (west), the name of the Lord "is great among the nations" (1:11). As a pure offering, incense is offered everywhere in the name of the Lord. The Lord's name is great among the nations, but the priests, who should know better, profane it by defiling the Lord 's table and spurning its food. Frustrating the Lord by complaining about the burden of the law concerning their sacrifice, the people bring animals that are mutilated, lame, or sick as offerings. The Lord asks if they really believe such offerings to be acceptable. The Lord curses those who vowed to offer a healthy male but who cheat by offering a defective one from their flock. The Lord reminds the priests that nations honor the Lord, the great king.

In chapter 2, the Lord threatens to send a curse on the priests if they do not listen to the command to give honor to the name of the Lord. In reality, the Lord declares the priests have already been cursed because they refuse to accept the law of the Lord in their hearts. The Lord will rebuke their offering and humiliate them by spreading dung on their faces, a reference to the dung of the many animals brought for sacrifice on major feasts. The Lord will treat them like dung, throwing them out in the refuse.

The Lord declares the reason for sending the command concerning sacrifice was so the covenant the Lord made with Levi might endure. Although the Lord made a covenant with Phinehas, the grandson of Aaron who belonged to the family of Levi, the Bible nowhere speaks of the Lord making a covenant with Levi. According to the current passage, the covenant was mutual, bringing life and peace to the offspring of Levi in response to the reverence and awe he showed for the Lord. Levi was reliable, with no falsehood on his lips, walking with the Lord in integrity and justice, turning many away from evil. In the same manner, the priests' lips safeguard knowledge of the law of the Lord and instruct the people as messengers of the Lord.

The Lord accuses the priests of turning aside from the way of Levi, causing many to stumble by their teachings. By their false teachings, they have corrupted the covenant of Levi. For this reason, the Lord made them contemptible and lowly before the people because they did not keep the commands of the Lord but showed in their instructions partiality toward those they favored.

Lectio Divina

Spend 8 to 10 minutes in silent contemplation of the following passage:

There is an old story about a man who received ten apples from the Lord. He received three apples to buy food, three for clothing, and three for shelter. The tenth apple was to be given to God. After spending the first nine apples, the man looked at the apple given for God, and it looked so tempting, he ate the apple and gave the core to God. This story illustrates further the message found in Malachi. God gave the people an abundant harvest and an ample amount of animals to provide food, clothing, and shelter. Unfortunately, the people gave God the core of all they received. They selected useless animals instead of healthy ones and offered them for sacrifice. The Lord became angry and refused to accept the sacrifices the people offered.

✠ *What can I learn from this passage?*

Day 4: Marriage and Divorce (Malachi 2:10—3)

Acknowledging the Israelites have one father, one God, the author questions why the people are unfaithful to each other, discarding the covenant of their ancestors. Judah, Jerusalem, and Israel have all performed the abominable act of rejecting the Lord. Judah profaned the Lord's holy place and married a "daughter of a foreign god" (2:11). On their return from exile, many of the people brought wives who worshiped false gods. The prophet pictures the Lord as cutting off the man who marries a woman who worships a foreign god and who makes an offering to the Lord of hosts.

The people mourn because the Lord no longer accepts their offering in a favorable light, and they ask, "Why?" The Lord stands as a witness between the man and the wife of his youth with whom he has broken faith. The man's wife is the true companion, the covenanted wife. Malachi states the Lord is the one who made them one, one flesh and one spirit. From this comes Godly offspring. The people are to be on guard for their life and not break faith with the wife of their youth.

The Lord God declares, "I hate divorce" (2:16). The Lord also expresses hatred for violence. The Lord warns the people should be on guard for their lives and not break faith with the Lord.

The prophet again adds his own commentary when he informs the people they have wearied the Lord. When the people ask how they have wearied the Lord, the prophet responds they joined with evildoers, saying they are good in the sight of the Lord, who is pleased with them, or they ask where this just God is, as though God does not care about their actions.

In chapter 3, the Lord speaks of sending a messenger who will prepare the way for the coming of the Lord. Although it is not clear who the messenger is in this passage, Matthew, in his Gospel, will use the passage to point to John the Baptist as the messenger who is to prepare the way of the Lord, namely Jesus (see Matthew 11:10). In 2:7, Malachi speaks of the descendants of Levi, the priests of Jerusalem, as the messenger of the Lord of hosts. In the current passage, the messenger of the Lord could refer to a human being or a divine person who brings a message from the Lord. Malachi declares the Lord, whom the people seek, will come suddenly into the Temple.

After portraying the Lord as the one speaking in verse 1, Malachi speaks about the Lord in verses 3 and 4 as though it is a commentary on what is happening. He asks who will be able to endure the day of the Lord's coming. The Lord will appear like a refiner's fire, like fullers' lye, purifying the Levites, refining them like gold or silver so they may bring offerings to the Lord in justice. When this happens, the offerings of Judah and Jerusalem will be pleasing to the Lord as it was in ancient days.

In verse 5, the Lord speaks again, promising swift punishment for the sorcerers, adulterers, and perjurers who deprive workers of their wages, oppress a widow or an orphan, or reject a resident alien with no thought of God. The Lord does not change, always remaining faithful to the covenant. The offspring of Jacob (Israelites) have rejected the Lord's statutes, but they continue to exist.

The Lord begs them to come back so the Lord can return to them. When the people ask why they should return, the Lord accuses them of robbing God. They then ask how they have robbed God. The Lord accuses them of robbing tithes and contributions belonging properly to the Lord, and for this the Lord curses them. In recompense, the Lord directs the people to bring the whole tithe into the storehouse so there will be food in the house of God. The Lord will then open the floodgates of heaven and pour down an abundance of blessings upon them. With the promise to keep the locusts from destroying their crops, the Lord declares the vine will not be barren. When all the nations see what the Lord has done, they will refer to the nation of Judah as blessed and their land delightful.

The words of the people overwhelm the Lord. They protest it is useless to serve the Lord, following the Lord's commands, and living as though they are mourning their sinfulness, since they gain nothing from it. Instead, the people call the arrogant blessed, noting evildoers not only prosper but also test God with no consequences.

The Lord listened to those who spoke together with reverence toward the Lord, and their names appear in a record book of the Lord. The ancients viewed the record book as a book containing the names of the faithful. They will belong to the Lord when the Lord acts. The Lord will show compassion for them as a father shows compassion for a faithful son. The Lord speaks of the contrast between the good and the evil on the day of the coming of the Lord. People will be able to distinguish the just from the wicked, the one who serves the Lord and the one who does not. For the arrogant and the wicked, the day will come like a blazing oven, leaving them like stubble without roots or branches. For those who serve the Lord faithfully, the sun of justice will arise with healing in its wings. The just will leap like calves from their stalls and tread down the wicked, who will become like dust under their feet.

The Lord calls upon the just to remember the law which the Lord gave to Moses on Mount Horeb (Sinai). The Lord will be sending Elijah to them before the great and terrible Judgment Day (the day of the Lord). The Second

Book of Kings makes no mention of Elijah's death but describes him as being taken up to heaven in a whirlwind (2 Kings 2:11). The Lord declares Elijah will come and turn the hearts of fathers and sons to each other as a sign of peace and glory in the land, thus averting the utter destruction which the Lord would bring. Many Jews await the return of Elijah, literally accepting this passage concerning the return of Elijah before the terrible judgment. The Gospels, with the exception of Luke, identify John the Baptist as sent in the spirit of Elijah.

Lectio Divina

Spend 8 to 10 minutes in silent contemplation of the following passage:

> Matthew seems to portray Jesus as saying John the Baptist is Elijah when he declares, "And if you are willing to accept it, he is Elijah, the one who is to come" (Matthew 11:14). He also points to John as the one who is the messenger sent to prepare the way of the Lord (see Matthew 11:9–10). Whether or not Malachi viewed his prophesy as pertaining to the coming of John in preparation for the Messiah, Matthew, under the inspiration of the Holy Spirit, makes this connection, showing the Lord's faithfulness to the covenant. Malachi tells us the Lord does not change, meaning the Lord will always remain faithful to the covenant, whether the people break their part of the covenant or not. The Lord God is the same universal Lord found in the Old and New Testaments.

✠ *What can I learn from this passage?*

Review Questions

1. What does the Lord say about the shepherds of the people of Judah?
2. Why does the Lord promise to save Judah first, before Jerusalem?
3. What does the Lord say about the false prophets?
4. Why did the Lord allow Jerusalem to be devastated and later restored?

About the Author

William A. Anderson, DMin, PhD, is a presbyter of the Diocese of Wheeling-Charleston, West Virginia. A director of retreats and parish missions, professor, catechist, spiritual director, and a former pastor, he has written extensively on pastoral, spiritual, and religious subjects. Father Anderson earned his doctor of ministry degree from St. Mary's Seminary & University in Baltimore, and his doctorate in sacred theology from Duquesne University in Pittsburgh.

CPSIA information can be obtained at www.ICGtesting.com
Printed in the USA
LVOW06s0106050514

384315LV00003B/3/P

9 780764 821370